UNDERSTANDING
Everyday Australian

Book Three

*A focus on spoken language
with language reviews, exercises and answers*

Susan Boyer

Boyer Educational Resources 2007
Reprinted 2008, 2009, 2011, 2013, 2014, 2016

Boyer Educational Resources
PO Box 255, Glenbrook 2773
Phone/fax (02) 47391538

Acknowledgments:
I would like to express my thanks to the following people for their contribution to the final presentation of this book:

I am very grateful to the teachers who trialed material contained in this book. In particular I'd like to thank Annette Macrae, Thérèse Murphy, Alison Hey and Sheila Addison for their involvement and constructive comments. I'd like to thank UWS College, Westmead for allowing me to trial the material in this book as a self-access resource with their English language students.

I wish to say thank you to James Greenhalgh, Clinton Bagley, Len Boyer and Jeanette Christian for their contribution to the accompanying audio recording. I'd also like to express my thanks to Jeanette Christian for her careful proofreading. Again, I want to thank my husband, Len, for the many hours spent working on the production of this book. His encouragement and interest has been a tremendous support throughout the project.

I wish to acknowledge Matthew Larwood for many of the illustrations used in this book. Cover illustrations & illustrations on pages 8, 15, 16, 41, 56 (2 & 5), 63, 66 (1,2 & 4), 77, 87, 90 (2), 111 are by Matthew J Larwood.

And last but not least, I am indebted to the many students who gave me insight into the needs of English language learners, studying in Australia.

Photographs on pages 42 & 51 - 53 were provided courtesy of Clean Up the World Ltd.

Images used herein were obtained from IMSI's MasterClips Collection, 1895 Francisco Blvd. East, San Rafael, CA 94901-5506, USA, as well as from Microsoft's Clip Gallery Ver 4.0 & Microsoft Pty Ltd, 65 Epping Road, North Ryde, NSW, Australia.

The kookaburra clip art was obtained from Australian Graphics Selection, New Horizons, Armidale, Australia.

National Library of Australia
Cataloguing-in-Publication data:

Boyer, Susan
Understanding Everyday Australian - Book Three: a focus on spoken language with language reviews, exercises and answers.

ISBN 978 1 877074 20 2
1. English language - Spoken English - Australia - Textbooks for foreign speakers.
2. English language - Spoken English - Australia - Problems, exercises, etc. I.
   Boyer, Leonard, 1951- . II. Title.

428.34

NOTE TO STUDENTS

Dear English language student,

Welcome to *Understanding Everyday Australian - Book Three*. This book, along with its accompanying audio recording, has been designed to help you to understand English as it is spoken in everyday situations in Australia. As a student of English, I am sure you are aware of the difference between the formally presented language of many textbooks and the speech you hear in your daily activities and conversations with Australians.

Using this book, along with its accompanying audio recording, you will discover the meaning of many widely used everyday expressions. The book also focuses on aspects of spoken English which are employed by native speakers every day. For example, you will learn expressions for agreeing and disagreeing politely; for answering a business phone call, negotiating a deal and for declining an invitation. You will also practise listening for important aspects of English pronunciation such as the contracting and linking of words in conversational speech. Additionally, aspects of grammar such as the use of articles, pronouns and phrasal verbs are demonstrated within the context of the conversations in this book. There is a list of language terms on pages 6 - 7 to help you understand words used to explain English grammar and pronunciation.

In some units of this book you are asked to check words in a dictionary, so have a good dictionary nearby while you are studying. Because English words are not always pronounced as they are spelt, you will also need to use a dictionary to learn the correct pronunciation. *A **good** dictionary will give clear examples of pronunciation and a pronunciation key*. The Pronunciation Key (usually at the front of the dictionary) will show symbols used for different sounds.

Pronunciation Note
Many dictionaries use the same pronunciation symbols as the **PHONEMIC CHART** at the back of this book. However, some dictionaries use different symbols, so it's important to check which symbols *your* dictionary uses.

I sincerely hope you enjoy and benefit from using *Understanding Everyday Australian - Book Three.*

Susan Boyer

NOTE TO TEACHERS

In order to maximise the benefit of this material in a classroom situation, it is highly recommended that you complement the material with the activities, reviews, discussions and role plays provided in the Teacher's Book. **Assessment checklists** and **feedback sheets** are also provided in the Teacher's Book. See back cover for details.

ABOUT THIS BOOK

Understanding Everyday Australian - Book Three has been designed so that you can work through it alone, without the help of a teacher, or in a classroom situation with other students. The book contains nine units, each based on a conversation about a particular topic. The units are divided into ***six parts*** which have been designed to introduce unfamiliar language, ***step by step,*** in a gradual and systematic way. The layout of the book is as follows:

Part 1 - Focus on listening for general understanding

Part 1 introduces the topic and invites you to listen to an everyday conversation and answer a few general questions by putting a tick next to the correct answers. You will be listening for ***general*** understanding of the conversation only. (You will not need to understand every word the first time you listen). This is an important step as it will help you to realise that it's not always necessary to hear every word to understand the general meaning of a conversation. In some units, you are asked to check words in a dictionary, so have a dictionary nearby when you are studying.

Part 2 - Focus on reading & finding the meaning

In this section, you will ***read*** Conversation 1 as you listen again. When you have finished listening, your task is to ***compare Conversation 1 with Conversation 2*** (which will be on the page next to Conversation 1). Conversation 1 contains the everyday expressions and Conversation 2 contains an interpretation of the expressions in Conversation 1. This section will help you to learn the ***meaning*** of the everyday expressions.

Part 3 - Focus on listening for detail

Now you will listen to Conversation 1 again and write in the missing words in the spaces as you hear them. Don't worry about spelling as this exercise focuses on your ***listening skills***. Listen to the conversation as many times as you like, then check your answers (and spelling) by comparing what you have written with Conversation 1.

Part 4 - Focus on writing for reinforcement

This section reinforces (strengthens) your memory as you listen once more to Conversation 1 and tick the newly learnt everyday expressions on the list as you hear them. Then you are asked to look at the list of expressions (all taken from Conversation 1) and try to remember their meaning. Write in the ones that you can remember, then check your answers by reading Conversation 1 again or checking the reference list at the back of the book. This may seem like hard work but ***writing*** the meanings of the newly learnt expressions is a useful way of reinforcing what you have just heard and read.

Part 5 - Focus on revision

Now it's time to test yourself and see what you have learnt by trying the language review. In this section, you are asked to use the newly learnt expressions in a different context. Firstly, you are asked to complete sentences with an appropriate expression and then complete a crossword. The answers to the crosswords can be found in the back of the book.

Part 6 - Focus on spoken language

This section focuses on other aspects of spoken English which make it difficult for learners to understand native speakers. Each unit highlights and explains a particular aspect of pronunciation, sentence structure or a conversation strategy which was used by the speakers in Conversation 1 of that unit. In this section, there will be exercises for you to complete to help you understand, learn and remember.

Language Reviews

After Unit 3, Unit 6 and Unit 9, you will find a language review which consists of the recently introduced expressions and pictures for you to match together. This will help you to see how much you have remembered. Don't worry if you make a mistake - you are still learning.

Answers
Answers to all exercises can be found in this section.

Reference Lists
The colloquial expressions used in the conversations of each unit are listed, along with their meanings, in the order that they occur in the conversations.

Note:
The meaning given to an expression in the reference lists, relates to the context in which it is used in the corresponding unit. There may be different meanings of a particular expression when that expression is used in a different context.

IMPORTANT NOTE TO STUDENTS

Please be aware that the meaning of colloquial language is *very dependent on the context or situation in which it is used.* 'Understanding Everyday Australian' has been designed to *introduce and explain* the meaning of colloquial expressions used by English speakers in the everyday situations presented in this book. However, because colloquial expressions can have different meanings in different situations, it is not advisable that students of Australian English immediately begin using the newly introduced expressions indiscriminately. It would be much better to spend time listening, recognising, and understanding the correct meaning of expressions in different situations *before you use them* in your conversations. Therefore, the author and publisher of this book will not be responsible to any person, with regard to the misuse of language, caused directly or indirectly by the information presented in this book.

UNDERSTANDING EVERYDAY AUSTRALIAN – BOOK 3

CONTENTS

CONTENTS

GLOSSARY OF LANGUAGE TERMS

Use this list as a reference while you are using this book.

adjective

An adjective is a word that describes **things**, (eg. *black* car); **people**, (eg. *beautiful* girl,) **places**, (eg. *crowded* city) or **events**, (eg. *exciting* race). See page 26 for examples of adjectives ending in 'ed' and 'ing'.

alphabet

The English alphabet consists of twenty six letters:
a, b, c, d, e, f, g, h, i, j, k, l, m, n, o, p, q, r, s, t, u, v, w, x, y, z.

These letters are categorised into **vowels**: a, e, i, o, u.
and **consonants**: b, c, d, f, g, h, j, k, l, m, n, p, q, r, s, t, v, w, x, y, z.
(The consonant letter 'y' can be pronounced as a vowel sound; for example: 'gym'.)

article

The words *'a'*, *'an'*, *'the'*, are called articles. '*The*' is referred to as the definite article. See page 49 for an explanation of the definite article.

auxiliary verb

An auxiliary is a 'helper' verb which is used with another verb to form tense, eg. *will* come, *did* come, *have* come. Modal auxiliary verbs are used with another verb to show mood or manner, eg. *should* come, *might* come, *must* come.

discourse marker

Discourse markers **show connection** between what has already been said and what will come next in a conversation, eg. 'Yes *and I'm sure you'll agree that...*' A discourse marker is also a word or expression which shows the speaker's attitude to what is being said, eg. '*Mm maybe, but...*' See details and examples on page 89.

ellipsis

The term 'ellipsis' refers to the omission of words from a sentence when the meaning is clear without them due to the context of the conversation. eg. *Ready?* meaning '*Are you* ready?' See page 108 for more examples of ellipsis.

noun

Nouns are words that name **things**, eg. car, house; **places**, eg. park, ocean; **people**, eg. John, sister; **abstract things** (things we can't see but can experience and talk about), eg. history, pain, ideas, education.

participle

The term participle refers to the form of a verb that ends in 'ed' or 'ing' to show past or present tenses; sometimes words ending with 'ed' and 'ing' act as adjectives. See page 26 for examples.

There are also some participles, used for verb tenses that have an irregular spelling. For examples of irregular verb participles, see page 75.

phrasal verb

When a verb is followed by one or two other words to form a particular meaning, these combinations are called 'phrasal verbs', eg. 'pick up', 'try on'. See page 54 for further explanation. See pages 55 & 109 for some examples of 'phrasal verbs'.

phonemic symbols

Phonemic symbols, sometimes called **sound symbols**, represent the sounds of English. English sounds are generally divided into two main categories: **vowel** sounds, and **consonant** sounds. The vowel sounds can be further divided into simple vowel sounds and **diphthong** sounds. Diphthongs can be defined as 'two vowel sounds linked or glided together within a syllable'. The **Phonemic Chart of English Sounds**, found at the back of this book, shows the sound symbols of English, along with example words to demonstrate each sound.

pronoun

A pronoun is a word which is used in place of a person, eg. *he, she, me, they*; or a word used in place of a thing, eg. *it*.

reflexive pronoun

Words such as *myself, yourself, ourselves, yourselves* are called reflexive pronouns. See page 86 - 87 for an explanation and examples.

schwa

The phonemic symbol ə, and the sound it represents, are referred to as 'schwa'. The symbol ə (schwa) is used in most dictionaries to represent weak, unstressed syllables in words. For example, the pronunciation of the word 'seven' is shown in most dictionaries as /sevən/ as the second syllable is weak and unstressed.

Note: The pronunciation of words is shown in dictionaries between two lines / /.
See page 15, Part 6A for more examples of weak sounds in spoken English.

GLOSSARY OF LANGUAGE TERMS

sentence stress   Words that carry the main message of the sentence contain *stressed* or strong syllables. Stressing the important words helps the listener to hear the message of the speaker. eg. I *want* to go **home**.

word stress   In words with more than one syllable, one sound is usually stronger (spoken more clearly) than the others. The term, **stressed syllable**, refers to the strongest (primary) sound in words of more than one syllable.

syllable   Spoken words are formed with **syllables**, meaning **units of sound**.
A syllable is a unit of sound, generally containing a vowel sound.
For example: well = one syllable; welcome = two syllables; unwelcome = three syllables

verb   A verb is a word which shows **action**: eg. He **ran** all the way.
or **experience**: eg. I **feel** cold. I **heard** a knock.
or **condition**: eg. She **is** a student. I **am** sick.

verb tenses   Tenses show the **time** of an action, event or condition. Some examples are:

past simple tense: indicates finished past action. eg. He *went* to Asia last year.

past perfect tense: used when telling a story about a period of time in the past and we want to talk about an event before that time in the past. We use 'had'+ past participle. See page 75.

Compare *past simple*
with *past perfect* tense: She *wrote* another book last year.

Only two years earlier she *had written* her first book.

present perfect tense: a) used for an action/experience which began in the past and has continued to the present. We use 'have' or 'has' + past participle. See page 75.

eg. I *have lived* here since 1998. eg. 1998 ← now

b) used when a past action/experience (which happened at an unspecified time) has present significance.

eg.. He *has been* to Asia.

present simple tense: a) indicates a present condition/fact.

eg. I *am* hungry. eg.

b) indicates a present routine. eg. I *work* four days each week. eg.

present continuous: (also called present progressive) a verb form made with *am/are/is* +...*ing*.

a) This tense is used to talk about an action which is happening at the time of speaking. eg. We *are waiting* for him.

b) The present progressive is also used to refer to a future arrangement.
eg. He *is leaving* tomorrow.

future simple tense: will + verb indicates future time, eg. I think, it *will rain* tomorrow.

NOTE:
This list is not intended as a complete guide. Refer to a comprehensive grammar book for more details.

UNIT 1

OTHER CULTURES

When people from different cultures and language backgrounds try to communicate, sometimes there can be misunderstandings. Why do you think this happens?
In this unit you will listen to a conversation between friends who are talking about a misunderstanding with someone from another culture. (Unit 1 on your audio recording.)

Part 1 - Pre Listening

Before listening, check the following words in a dictionary. Match each to its correct meaning. You can check your answers on page 112.

misunderstand	personal	unacceptable	embarrassed	abrupt

1. not OK, not acceptable _____ 2. private _____

3. in a rude way, speaking too directly _____ 4. not understand_____

5. feel worried and ashamed because of something that happened _____

Listening for general understanding

The conversation contains 'everyday' expressions that will be explained later in the unit, so don't worry if you don't understand every word. This time you are listening for general understanding of the topic. As you listen, tick the correct answers below. Then check your answers on page 112.

1) When Don's neighbours first arrived next door, he thought:

> a) they were friendly
>
> b) they were abrupt and unfriendly

2) What did the neighbours do when Don had car trouble?

> a) They offered help.
>
> b) They called the police.

3) A few weeks after the car trouble, what did Don's neighbours ask?

> a) why he didn't have children
>
> b) if they could borrow money.

4) What did Don explain to his neighbours about their question?

> a) It was interesting.
>
> b) It's considered to be personal and we don't ask those questions.

Now we'll look at the everyday expressions used in the conversation – turn to the next page.

CONVERSATION 1 (with everyday expressions)

◀◀ **Replay Conversation 1**
Read this conversation as you listen to the audio recording. Do you know what the _underlined_ words mean? They are colloquial or everyday expressions.

Kara: So **how are things** with your neighbours these days Don?

Don: We're getting on **like a house on fire** now. It took a while to **break the ice** but we're getting on well now.

Kara: Good to hear. I remember you **didn't get off to a good start**.

Don: Mm I remember. We **didn't hit it off** when they first moved next door. I thought they **came across as** abrupt and unfriendly.

Kara: So what happened to change things?

Don: Well, one day, when we had trouble with our car, they were there **in a flash** to offer help. So **it dawned on me** that I'd misunderstood their way of speaking. I'd thought they were unfriendly but it was just a different way of speaking. It was a cultural thing.

Kara: Yes, I know what you mean. It's easy to **get the wrong idea about** people sometimes; especially because of cultural differences.

Don: Yes. It's funny. A few weeks after the car trouble, we were **having a chat** over the fence when they asked my wife and I why we didn't have any children. I was quite **taken aback** at first and I thought they'd really **overstepped the mark**. Then I realised it was a cultural thing again, so I just explained to them that we consider that sort of thing to be personal and we don't usually ask those sorts of questions.

Kara: And what did they say to that?

Don: Well, they were very embarrassed, of course, but they were really pleased that we'd explained the situation to them. They said there's no way of knowing about things like that unless someone tells them. Since then we've had a long conversation about **the dos and don'ts** in both our cultures.

Kara: Yeah. We've probably all **put our foot in it** at some time because we didn't understand another person's cultural background.

Don: Yeah well, the whole experience was **an eye opener** for me. For a start, it taught me not to **jump to conclusions** about people.

Kara: It'**s easier said than done** though, isn't it? We generally expect people to do things the way we do them and if they don't, we can think it's rudeness rather than seeing it as a cultural thing.

Don: Well, as I said, in future I'm going to try to **give people the benefit of the doubt**. **When all is said and done**, I think people everywhere are really more the same than different - in the important things anyway.

Kara: Yes, I'd have to agree with that.

Now let's see what these expressions mean - look at the next page.

CONVERSATION 2 (explanation of everyday expressions)

Compare Conversation 1 with Conversation 2 -You will see that some of the words are different but the meaning is the same in both conversations. Find the underlined words in Conversation 1, then underline the words with the same meaning in Conversation 2. For example: <u>how are things</u> (Conversation 1) = <u>how is your situation</u> (Conversation 2)

Kara: So <u>how is your situation</u> with your neighbours these days Don?

Don: We're getting on like very good friends now. It took a while to be relaxed and friendly but we're getting on well now.

Kara: Good to hear. I remember you didn't start well.

Don: Mm I remember. We didn't have a good relationship when they first moved next door. I thought they seemed to be abrupt and unfriendly.

Kara: So what happened to change things?

Don: Well, one day, when we had trouble with our car, they were there very quickly to offer help. So it became clear to me that I'd misunderstood their way of speaking. I'd thought they were unfriendly but it was just a different way of speaking. It was a cultural thing.

Kara: Yes, I know what you mean. It's easy to misunderstand people sometimes; especially because of cultural differences.

Don: Yes. It's funny. A few weeks after the car trouble, we were talking informally over the fence when they asked my wife and I why we didn't have any children. I was quite surprised and shocked at first and I thought they'd really behaved in an unacceptable way. Then I realised it was a cultural thing again, so I just explained to them that we consider that sort of thing to be personal and we don't usually ask those sorts of questions.

Kara: And what did they say to that?

Don: Well, they were very embarrassed, of course, but they were really pleased that we'd explained the situation to them. They said there's no way of knowing about things like that unless someone tells them. Since then we've had a long conversation about things you should do and things you shouldn't do in both our cultures.

Kara: Yeah. We've probably all said or done something embarrassing at some time because we didn't understand another person's cultural background.

Don: Yeah well, the whole experience was a situation to learn from for me. For a start, it taught me <u>not</u> to form an opinion before having enough information about people.

Kara: It sounds easy to do but is difficult to do though, isn't it? We generally expect people to do things the way we do them and if they don't, we can think it's rudeness rather than seeing it as a cultural thing.

Don: Well, as I said, in future I'm going to try to believe people are acting honestly, even if I'm not sure. When everything is considered, I think people everywhere are really more the same than different - in the important things anyway.

Kara: Yes, I'd have to agree with that.

> Now to become familiar with the everyday expressions, practise reading CONVERSATION 1 aloud with a partner.

◂◂ **Replay Conversation 1**

Listen to the conversation again and write in the missing words. You may need to listen more than once. Don't worry about your spelling as this activity focuses on listening skills; you can check your spelling later.)

Kara: So <u>how are things</u> with your neighbours these days Don?

Don: We're getting on <u>like a _____</u> on fire now. It took a while to <u>break the _____</u> but we're getting on well now.

Kara: Good to hear. I remember you <u>didn't get _____</u> to a good start.

Don: Mm I remember. We <u>didn't _____ it off</u> when they first moved next door. I thought they <u>came _____</u> as abrupt and unfriendly.

Kara: So what happened to change things?

Don: Well, one day, when we had trouble with our car, they were there<u>_____ a flash</u> to offer help. So <u>it dawned _____ me</u> that I'd misunderstood their way of speaking. I'd thought they were unfriendly but it was just a different way of speaking. It was a cultural thing.

Kara: Yes, I know what you mean. It's easy to <u>get the wrong _____</u> about people sometimes; especially because of cultural differences.

Don: Yes. It's funny. A few weeks after the car trouble, we were <u>having a _____</u> over the fence when they asked my wife and I why we didn't have any children. I was quite <u>taken aback</u> at first and I thought they'd really <u>overstepped the _____</u>. Then I realised it was a cultural thing again, so I just explained to them that we consider that sort of thing to be personal and we don't usually ask those sorts of questions.

Kara: And what did they say to that?

Don: Well, they were very embarrassed, of course, but they were really pleased that we'd explained the situation to them. They said there's no way of knowing about things like that unless someone tells them. Since then we've had a long conversation about <u>the ____ and don'ts</u> in both our cultures.

Kara: Yeah. We've probably all <u>put our _____ in it</u> at some time because we didn't understand another person's cultural background.

Don: Yeah well, the whole experience was <u>an _____ opener</u> for me. For a start, it taught me not to <u>_____ to conclusions</u> about people.

Kara: It<u>'s easier _____ than done</u> though, isn't it? We generally expect people to do things the way we do them and if they don't, we can think it's rudeness rather than seeing it as a cultural thing.

Don: Well, as I said, in future I'm going to try to <u>give people the benefit of the _____</u>. <u>When all is _____ and done</u>, I think people everywhere are really more the same than different – in the important things anyway.

Kara: Yes, I'd have to agree with that.

> Now check your answers by comparing this page with CONVERSATION 1.

In order to become more familiar with these new everyday expressions:

◀◀ Replay Conversation 1

   1) Listen and tick the boxes ☑ next to the expressions as you hear them.

   2) Write the definitions you can remember. (Some have been done for you as examples.)

   3) Check your answers by turning to page 124.

☐ how are things........................	how is your situation
☐ like a house on fire.....................	_____
☐ break the ice...............................	_____
☐ didn't get off to a good start...........	_____
☐ didn't hit it off...........................	_____
☐ came across as...........................	_____
☐ in a flash..................................	_____
☐ it dawned on me.........................	_____
☐ get the wrong idea about..............	_____
☐ having a chat.............................	_____
☐ taken aback...............................	_____
☐ overstepped the mark...................	_____
☐ the dos and don'ts......................	_____
☐ put our foot in it.........................	_____
☐ an eye opener............................	_____
☐ jump to conclusions...............	_____
☐ easier said than done...................	_____
☐ give (people) the benefit of the doubt	_____
☐ when all is said and done..............	_____

LANGUAGE NOTE

* When we use the expression, 'It's funny...' (as in line 13 of Conversation 1) before telling a story, it can mean 'It's surprising' or 'It's a situation that's difficult to explain.'

* Pronouns, when used in expressions, can usually be substituted with different pronouns.
  For example: 'got on _your_ nerves' can also be '_got on my/his/her/my/our nerves_'
            'it dawned on _me_' can also be ' _it dawned on him/her/us/them_'
            '_put our_ foot in it' can also be '_put his/her/my/their foot in it_'

CROSSWORD - LANGUAGE REVIEW

Complete the sentences, choosing from the everyday expressions that are listed below. You can use the clues in brackets ( ) at the end of each sentence to help you. Then complete the crossword using the everyday expressions you have written. One has been done as an example.

~~easier said than done~~	benefit of the doubt	eye opener
have a chat	put my foot in it	house on fire	get the wrong idea
break the ice	jump to conclusions	in a flash

ACROSS

1) Saving money for my holiday is <u>easier</u> <u>said</u> <u>than</u> <u>done</u>. (easy to say but difficult to do)

3) When meeting people for the first time, don't _____ ___ _____ about them. (form an opinion before having enough information)

5) I ____ ____ _____ ____ ____ when I said he's too old to drive. (said an embarrassing thing)

7) He said he didn't take the car so I gave him the _____ ___ _____ _____ (believed him)

9) My friend and I _____ ___ _____ on the phone once a week. (talk informally)

DOWN

2) It's easy to _____ _____ _____ _____; if you don't listen carefully. (misunderstand)

4) When he heard about the accident, he was there ____ __ _____. (very quickly)

6) When John and I met, we got on like a _____ ___ _____ immediately. (as very good friends)

8) A smile will usually _____ _____ _____ between people. (make a relaxed situation)

10) Travelling to another country was an _____ _____ for me. (a situation to learn from)

Answers, page 112.

FOCUS ON SPOKEN LANGUAGE

A) Noticing 'weak forms' in spoken English

In naturally spoken English, some words are often pronounced with a weak pronunciation and therefore can be difficult to hear. These include words such as 'a', 'are, 'to', 'you', 'your' 'and', 'of'.

1) Look at Kara's question. ——→ Write the words you think are missing from Kara's question.

> So how _____ things with _____ neighbours these days Don?

◄◄ Replay Conversation 1

Now listen to the first line of Conversation 1 and check your answers above. As you listen, notice the weak pronunciation of the words you have written. You can also check the answers on page 112.

When words are pronounced with a weak sound, they are referred to as **weak forms**.
The part of a word with a weak sound is generally represented in dictionaries with the symbol ə.

2) Now listen to Don's reply to Kara (2nd line of Conversation 1) and complete the missing words.

> _____ getting on like a house on fire now. It took a while to break the ice but _____ getting on well now.

You can check the answers on page 112.

Contractions

When speaking in a natural, fluent, conversational way, English speakers (including educated speakers) contract and link words to help the smooth flow of speech.

Speakers often use 'contractions'. This means they link two words together into one word.
For example, instead of saying, *We are getting on well now,* Don said, *We're getting on well now.*

we're is the contracted form of 'we are'

When contracted words are written, an apostrophe (') is used to show where letters in the word have been left out.

eg. We are ——→	We're	The apostrophe ' shows that the letter 'a' in 'are' is missing.
did not ——→	didn't	The apostrophe ' shows that the letter 'o' in 'not' is missing.
I had ——→	I'd	The apostrophe ' shows that the letters 'ha' in 'had' are missing.

◄◄ Replay Conversation 1

3) Read and listen to Conversation 1 again and highlight the contractions used in the conversation (page 10) as you read the conversation. Notice the way the contractions are pronounced. Notice the correct position for the apostrophe ('). How many contractions did you find? Check your answers on page 112

Note: In addition to showing contractions, an apostrophe (') is also used to show that something belongs to someone. For example, in Conversation 1 (line 24) Kara talks about another person's culture.

B) *we're, were* and *where*

There are some words in English that have a similar pronunciation but the meaning or spelling is different. Look at the examples of these words in the following sentence.

- We *were* lost yesterday but next time *we're* going to take a map to check **where** we are going.

  Grammar Note: *were* is the past tense form of the plural verb *are*

  *we're** is the contracted form of *we are*

  where means *which place*

 *Pronunciation Note: we're is sometimes pronounced /wɪə/.

Read Don's part of Conversation 1 on page 10 and complete the sentences below with *were* or *we're*.

_____ getting on like a house on fire now. It took a while to break the ice but _____ getting on well now.

Well they _____ very embarrassed, of course, but they _____ really pleased that we'd explained the situation to them.

Further Practice – *were*, *where* or *we're*?

Complete the sentences below by writing the correct word (*were, where* or *we're*) in the appropriate space (using a capital letter where necessary).

1. _____ very happy with our English lessons.

2. We visited over ten countries while we _____ overseas last year.

3. When we _____ young, we _____ always in trouble.

4. When we have finished this course, _____ going to have a final exam.

5. _____ do you come from?

6. Yesterday we _____ all studying hard for the language tests.

Answers, page 113.

More examples of words that are pronounced similarly:

Look at the following sentences. The **bold** words in each sentence may be confused as they are pronounced similarly.

- **You're** learning quickly because you do **your** homework every night!

Grammar Note: **you're** is the contracted form of **you are**
your shows possession (the homework belongs to you)

- **They're** travelling **there** by taxi because **their** car was damaged in an accident.

Grammar Note: **they're** is a contracted form of **they are**.
their shows possession (the car belongs to them)
there shows in or at a particular place. When will they get **there**?

Spelling Practice

Complete the sentences below by choosing the correct word from the box and writing it in the appropriate space (using a capital letter where necessary). The underlined pronoun in each sentence will give you a clue about which words to use. You can check your answers on page 113.

their	they're	were	we're	you're	your

1) _____ car was stolen while <u>they</u> were away last week, and _____ still upset about it.

2) Yesterday we_____ worried about the exam but now_____ happy with our results.

3) _____brother is taller than you, even though _____ older than him.

C) 'A cultural thing'

The expression 'a cultural thing' is used in Conversation 1 (p. 10) to express the idea that the situation being spoken about involves or affects a particular group of people and doesn't involve or affect everyone. We usually use the expression to show why there has been a misunderstanding between groups of people.

Similar expressions are used to refer to other groups of people. Look at the examples below.

'Men don't understand…it's <u>a female thing</u>.'

'We understand what the manager means because it's <u>a company thing</u>.'

Note: The word 'thing' has a variety of meanings and is used in various ways.

For example, *'How're things?'* is used as a general greeting when friends meet, and means, 'How is your life in a general way since we last met?

- The expression, *'How are things with (something)?'* can be used to ask about a specific situation. For example, Kara used this question in Conversation 1 of this unit to ask Don about the specific situation with his neighbours.
  eg. *'So how're <u>things</u> with your neighbours these days Don? '*

- The expression, '*I have a thing* about (something)' is explained in Unit 5, Fears and Phobias, as meaning 'I really <u>don't like</u> (something)'. eg. *I <u>have a thing about</u> flying'* = *I really <u>don't like</u> flying*.

  However, the expression, '*I <u>have a thing about</u> (something)*' can also mean, 'I really <u>like</u> (something)'.

  eg. He has a <u>thing</u> about motorbikes; he has several of his own.

  Remember, the meaning will depend on the context of the conversation.

UNIT 2

SPORT AND HOBBIES

Can you name each of these activities?   You can check the answers on page 113.

In this Unit you will listen to a conversation between friends who are talking about their interests and hobbies (Unit 2 on your audio recording). The conversation contains everyday expressions that will be explained later in the unit - so don't worry if you don't understand every word. This time you are listening for general understanding of the topic.

Part 1 - Pre Listening

Before listening, match the following words with the definitions below.

be competitive	physically fit	participate	a team	extreme

1) have a strong desire to win _____ 2) a group of players _____

3) do, share in an activity _____ 4) unreasonable, too much _____

5) having a healthy body _____

Answers, page 113.

Listening for general understanding

Now listen to the conversation and answer the questions below:

A) Which of the activities, illustrated on the previous page, are mentioned in the conversation?

_____

◄◄ **Replay Conversation 1**

B) As you listen again, tick the correct answers below.

1) Kim (first speaker) invites Paul to go

        a) jogging

        b) fishing

2) Paul would like to

        a) play in a team sport

        b) learn to paint

3) The speakers think that when playing sport,

        a) people can be too competitive

        b) people should be more competitive

Answers, page 113.

> Now we'll look at the everyday expressions used in the conversation – turn to the next page.

CONVERSATION 1 (with everyday expressions)

◀◀ Replay Conversation 1

Read this conversation as you listen to the audio tape. Do you know what the <u>underlined</u> words mean? They are colloquial or everyday expressions.

Kim: Oh, Paul. We're going fishing this weekend, if you want to come along.

Paul: I heard you're really **into** fishing these days. Thanks all the same, but I'll **take a raincheck**.

Kim: OK but let me know if you want to go anytime. I'll **go at the drop of a hat**.

Paul: Thanks. I'll **keep it in mind**.

Kim: You know, I should have started fishing years ago. It's really helping me **unwind**.

Paul: It sounds like it! To be honest with you, fishing **doesn't do much for me**. I went fishing once but I was bored. If I **take up** a sport, it'll have to be something more active than fishing.

Kim: You mean something like jogging or cycling?

Paul: No, I'd prefer a team sport. **I wouldn't mind** taking up soccer again but **to tell you the truth**, I don't think I'm **up to it** now.

Kim: I didn't know you played soccer.

Paul: Yeah, I used to play every week but when I got busy at work I decided to **give it up**. Then later, when I had **time on my hands**, I started playing cards or chess with friends every week instead of playing sport again.

Kim: Well cards or chess are fine if it helps you unwind.

Paul: I know but I'm turning into **a couch potato**. I need to do something more active to **get into shape** again. I could **try my hand at** cricket or baseball, I guess.

Kim: Go for it, if that's what you'd like. I must say competitive sports don't interest me.

Paul: Why's that?

Kim: Well, if you're playing for a team, you have to take it seriously and **play by the book**. I'd prefer to **do my own thing**.

Paul: Mm. I know what you mean. People **go overboard** sometimes and become too competitive when it comes to sport. Then it gets too **full on** and that takes the fun out of it. I just want to do something to get back into shape - and hopefully have some fun at the same time.

Kim: Well it sounds like you've got the right idea.

Now let's see what these expressions mean - look at the next page.

CONVERSATION 2 (explanation of everyday expressions)

Compare Conversation 1 with Conversation 2 -You will see that some of the words are different but the meaning is the same in both conversations. Find the underlined words in Conversation 1, then underline the words with the same meaning in Conversation 2. For example: <u>right into</u> (Conversation 1) = <u>very involved in</u> (Conversation 2)

Kim: Oh, Paul. We're going fishing this weekend, if you want to come along.

Paul: I heard you're <u>very involved in</u> fishing these days. Thanks all the same, but I'll say no to this invitation (but may accept at another time).

Kim: OK but let me know if you want to go anytime. I'll go willingly, immediately, without hesitation.

Paul: Thanks. I'll remember that.

Kim: You know, I should have started fishing years ago. It's really helping me relax.

Paul: It sounds like it! To be honest with you, fishing doesn't interest or excite me. I went fishing once but I was bored. If I start participating in a sport, it'll have to be something more active than fishing.

Kim: You mean something like jogging or cycling?

Paul: No, I'd prefer a team sport. I would like to (try) taking up soccer again but really, I don't think I'm capable or fit enough to do it now.

Kim: I didn't know you played soccer.

Paul: Yeah, I used to play every week but when I got busy at work I decided to quit, stop doing it. Then later, when I had some free time available, I started playing cards or chess with friends every week instead of playing sport again.

Kim: Well cards or chess are fine if it helps you unwind.

Paul: I know but I'm turning into an inactive, lazy person. I need to do something more active to become physically fit again. I could test my skill at cricket or baseball, I guess.

Kim: Go for it, if that's what you'd like. I must say competitive sports don't interest me.

Paul: Why's that?

Kim: Well, if you're playing for a team, you have to take it seriously and follow the rules. I'd prefer to do things the way I want to and be independent.

Paul: Mm. I know what you mean. People become extreme sometimes and become too competitive when it comes to sport. Then it gets too intense, extreme and that takes the fun out of it. I just want to do something to get back into shape - and hopefully have some fun at the same time.

Kim: Well it sounds like you've got the right idea.

> Now to become familiar with the everyday expressions, practise CONVERSATION 1 aloud with a partner.

◄◄ **Replay Conversation 1**
Listen to the conversation again and write in the missing words. You may need to listen more than once. (Don't worry about your spelling as this activity focuses on listening skills; you can check your spelling later.)

Kim: Oh, Paul. We're going fishing this weekend, if you want to come along.

Paul: I heard you're really_____fishing these days. Thanks all the same, but I'll <u>take a</u> _____check.

Kim: OK but let me know if you want to go anytime. I'll go <u>at the drop of a</u> _____.

Paul: Thanks. I'll _____ <u>it in mind</u>.

Kim: You know, I should have started fishing years ago. It's really helping me <u>unwind</u>.

Paul: It sounds like it! To be honest with you, fishing <u>doesn't</u>_____ <u>much for me</u>. I went fishing once but I was bored. If I _____ up a sport, it'll have to be something more active than fishing.

Kim: You mean something like jogging or cycling?

Paul: No, I'd prefer a team sport. I <u>wouldn't</u>_____ taking up soccer again but <u>to</u>_____ <u>you the truth,</u> I don't think I'm _____ <u>to it</u> now.

Kim: I didn't know you played soccer.

Paul: Yeah, I used to play every week but when I got busy at work I decided to _____ <u>it up</u>. Then later, when I had _____ <u>on my hands</u>, I started playing cards or chess with friends every week instead of playing sport again.

Kim: Well cards or chess are fine if it helps you unwind.

Paul: I know but I'm turning into <u>a couch</u> _____. I need to do something more active to <u>get into</u>_____ again. I could <u>try my</u>_____ <u>at</u> cricket or baseball, I guess.

Kim: Go for it, if that's what you'd like. I must say, competitive sports don't interest me.

Paul: Why's that?

Kim: Well, if you're playing for a team, you have to take it seriously and <u>play by the</u>_____. I'd prefer to <u>do my</u>_____ <u>thing</u>.

Paul: Mm. I know what you mean. People <u>go</u>_____ <u>board</u> sometimes and become too competitive when it comes to sport. Then it gets too <u>full</u>_____ and that takes the fun out of it. I just want to do something to get back into shape - and hopefully have some fun at the same time.

Kim: Well it sounds like you've got the right idea.

> Now check your answers by comparing this page with
> CONVERSATION 1.

In order to become more familiar with these new everyday expressions:

◀◀ **Replay Conversation 1**

   1) **Listen and tick the boxes** ☑ **next to the expressions as you hear them.**
   2) **Write the definitions you can remember. (Some have been done for you as examples.)**
   3) **Check your answers by turning to page 125.**

☐ into (something) ....   *very involved in (something)*

☐ take a raincheck.....................

☐ (go) at the drop of a hat..........

☐ keep it in mind....................

☐ unwind…….....................….

☐ doesn't do much for me..........

☐ take up (a sport)................

☐ I wouldn't mind ....

☐ to tell you the truth.................

☐ up to it.............................

☐ give (it) up.........................

☐ time on my hands................

☐ a couch potato.......................

☐ get into shape......................

☐ try my hand at ....

☐ play by the book ....

☐ do my own thing.................

☐ go overboard.....................

☐ full on..............................

LANGUAGE NOTE

   * The expression 'take up' (a sport) can be used to talk about an activity, interest or habit that someone starts doing. For example: 'I've <u>taken up</u> cooking', 'He's <u>taken up</u> smoking again.'

   * Where pronouns are used in the following expressions, they can be substituted with other pronouns. For example: 'time on *my* hands' can also be 'time on *his/her/our/their* hands'
             'do *my* own thing' can also be 'do *his/her/our/their* own thing'

CROSSWORD - LANGUAGE REVIEW

Complete the sentences, choosing from the everyday expressions that are listed below. You can use the clues in brackets ( ) at the end of each sentence to help you. Then complete the crossword using the everyday expressions you have written. The first one has been done as an example.

give up	couch potato	take up	~~try my hand at~~	time on my hands
unwind	drop of a hat	get into shape	a rain check	do my own thing

ACROSS

1) I'd like to **_try my hand at_** ice skating one day. I think it would be fun. (try, test my skill)

3) I work in my own business as I prefer to ___ ____ _____ _____ . (be independent)

5) I was a _____ _____ last weekend. I just watched TV all day. (an inactive person)

7) I had to _____ ___ jogging because my knees started to hurt. (quit/stop)

9) Sorry I can't go to the movies tonight but can I take __ _____ _____? (not go this time but accept the invitation at a future time)

DOWN

2) I want to ____ _____ _____ before summer. I think I'll go to a gym. (become physically fit)

4) I want to learn to play the piano when I have more_____ ___ ___ _____. (free time)

6) I would go back to England at the _____ ___ ___ _____ if I could. (willingly, immediately)

8) I usually _____ by having a cup of tea and reading a book. (relax)

10) I'd like to _____ ____ flying but it's very expensive. (start doing, participating in)

Answers, page 113

FOCUS ON SPOKEN LANGUAGE

A) Using the correct verb when talking about sport and hobbies.

We use specific verbs when referring to particular activities. For example:

	verb	verb	verb
We say:	I play soccer.	I go swimming.	I do pottery as a hobby.
	I play golf.	I go jogging.	I do the housework.

Can you see a general pattern?

We generally use '*play*' with a partner, group or team sport. eg. I *play* soccer.	We generally use '*go*' with sports or activities ending with '*ing*' eg. I *go* jogg*ing* each day.	We generally use '*do*' with individual hobbies or activities. eg. I *do* pottery as a hobby.

(Note: There are exceptions to these patterns).

Exercise 1) Add the activities in the box to the lists below:

archery	golf	gymnastics	bushwalking	bowling
surfing	tennis	cricket	cycling	skiing	fishing	origami
snooker	scuba diving	sight seeing	soccer	yoga

Verb Forms play/plays/playing/played	Verb Forms go/goes/going/went/have been	Verb Forms do/does/doing/did/have done
chess cards	jogging shopping	housework pottery

Exercise 2) Complete the following sentences with the correct verb form (past, present or future). One has been done as an example.

1) I _**play**_ soccer every weekend.

2) We _____ fishing again last weekend.

3) I'd like to _____ bushwalking in the mountains during the holidays.

4) We _____ golf every Saturday afternoon.

5) She _____ yoga every afternoon after work.

6) I think we'll _____ cycling when we go to Amsterdam. It's very flat there.

7) My brother _____ archery as a hobby.

8) Do you know how to _____ origami?

9) We plan to _____ scuba diving when we are on holiday in Queensland.

10) We _____ skiing in the Snowy Mountains last winter.

You can check your answers on page 114.

FOCUS ON SPOKEN LANGUAGE

B) Describing feelings and situations – adjectives ending with 'ed' and 'ing'

In Conversation 1, Paul described how he felt about fishing.

Check Conversation 1 (page 20) and complete the following sentence.

Paul: '...I went fishing once but _____.'

When describing feelings or experiences, we can use words ending in **ing** (bor**ing**) or **ed** (bor**ed**).

When used to <u>describe</u> something, these words act as adjectives eg. This is a bor*ing* lesson.

Grammar Note:

In grammar books, verbs ending in *ed* are called *past participles;* verbs ending in *ing* are called *present participles*. However, when used to *describe* something as in the examples on this page, they act as *adjectives*. See Glossary of Language Terms, page 6, for an explanation of 'adjective'.

Take care when using **ing** or **ed** adjectives, as they can convey different meanings.

1) Look at the pattern, then compare and complete the sentences:

To describe **how we are affected** or **how we feel about** something, we end the word with **ed**. eg. 'I am **confused** by this information.'	To describe **the person, thing or situation** which **gives the effect** to us, we end the word with **ing**. eg. This information is **confusing**.
1a) She was *amazed* by the story.	1b) The story was amaz**ing**.
2a) I feel relax**ed** at the beach.	2b) The beach is relax**ing**.
3a) I get bor**ed** at school.	3b) I think school is _____
4a) I get _____ when I study for too long.	4b) It's tir**ing** to study for too long.
5a) I was _____ by the movie.	5b) The movie was frighten**ing**.
6a) I get excit**ed** when I watch soccer.	6b) I think soccer is _____.

2) Complete the story below using the correct words from the box. Answers, page 114.

tired	tiring	~~exciting~~	excited	~~amazed~~	boring	bored	amazing

The sports competition was very **_exciting_**. Everyone in the audience was

cheering and clapping. We were all very _____ when the winner

was announced. I was **_amazed_** to see how fast the competitors could run.

Their speeds were _____!

The long speeches that followed the competition were a bit _____.

I often get _____ when people keep talking for a long time. In fact, I started to feel so _____,

I had trouble keeping my eyes open. It was a long and _____ day but it was a lot of fun.

C) Talking about attitudes and preferences

It is common in English for one verb to follow another verb.

This happens for example, when we talk about our attitude to an action.

For example: He **likes** **to play** soccer.

The first verb refers to the attitude. The second verb refers to the action.

He **likes**	**to play** soccer on the weekend.
She **loves**	**to go** skiing in winter.
I **prefer**	**to do** aerobics at the gym.
They **want**	**to go** sailing this summer.

*Note: In these sentences, the second verb is called *an infinitive*, eg. **to play**, **to go**, **to do**.

(The verb *enjoy* is not used before infinitives. ~~I enjoy to play tennis~~ is **not** correct.)

Some verbs are followed by the *ing* form of the verb.

For example: I **enjoy** **play*ing*** cards.

The **first verb** refers to the **attitude.** The **second verb** refers to the **action**.

I **enjoy**	**play*ing*** cards
I **love**	**go*ing*** fishing.
I **like**	**do*ing*** origami.
I **prefer**	**play*ing*** tennis.(rather than some other sport)

(Note: The verb *want* is not used with *ing* verbs. ~~I want going fishing~~ is **not** correct.)

We can also use the pattern:

verb	activity
I **enjoy**	tennis
I **love**	fishing.
I **like**	origami.
I **prefer**	tennis (used when comparing with other sports)

Practice

Using the <u>verb forms</u> in Part C write a few sentences about the sport or activities you enjoy.

I enjoy _____

_____   _____

DIET AND FITNESS

In this Unit you will listen to a conversation between friends who are talking about diet and fitness (Unit 3 on the audio recording). The conversation contains everyday expressions that will be explained later in the unit - so don't worry if you don't understand every word. This time you are listening for general understanding of the topic.

Part 1 - Pre Listening

Before listening, match the following words with the definitions below.
One has been done as an example. You can check your answers on page 115.

habits	products	label	~~snack~~	to inspire
	junk food		willpower	experts

1. a small amount of food that you can eat between main meals   _____snack_____

2. activities and actions that you do often and regularly   _____

3. food that is unhealthy but quick and easy to eat   _____

4. to make someone feel they want to do something   _____

5 strong control of your thoughts and decisions to do something   _____

6. things that are made to be sold   _____

7. information put on a product to tell you about the product   _____

8. people who have a lot of knowledge about something   _____

Listening for general understanding

Now listen to the conversation and tick the correct answers below.
You can check your answers on page 115.

1) Pam says that Sara looks:

        a) tired (not good)

        b) great (very good)

2) What does Sara do every morning now?

        a) has fruit for breakfast

        b) goes for a walk

        c) listens to music

3) Sara says it is important to:

        a) drink a lot of water

        b) read the labels on food

Now we'll look at the everyday expressions used in the conversation – turn to the next page.

CONVERSATION 1 (with everyday expressions)

◀◀ Replay Conversation 1

Read this conversation as you listen to the audio recording. Do you know what the _underlined_ words mean? They are colloquial or 'everyday' expressions.

Sara: Hi Pam. **Long time no see**. How are you?

Pam: Hi Sara. Good to see you. You look great!

Sara: Thanks. I've been on a **health kick** since the last time I saw you. You know - exercise program, special diet – **the works**.

Pam: A diet? But you didn't need to lose weight, did you?

Sara: I didn't really go on the diet to lose weight; it was about feeling better. Before the diet I was feeling really **burnt out**. I didn't have any **oomph**, or **get up and go**. Now I'm feeling **on top of the world**. I've never felt better.

Pam: Well the effort has **paid off**. You look really great. And you mentioned exercise. Did you go to the gym?

Sara: Yeah, I **worked out** at the gym in the beginning and it **got me off to a good start**. Now I go for a walk every morning before breakfast and it puts me in **a good frame of mind** for the rest of the day.

Pam: Wow. I should do something like that. Trouble is I don't have any will power **when it comes to** food. I plan to eat only healthy food but then I see something **yummy** and my good plans **go out the window**.

Sara: I know. I've done that too. As the saying goes: '**Old habits die hard**'. But really it's a matter of changing your **mindset** about what's yummy.

Pam: I know. I eat too much junk food and not enough **greens**.

Sara: Well I've learnt that healthy food doesn't have to be boring – it can be yummy too.

Pam: I guess so. But I get **bamboozled** when it comes to knowing what's best. There are a lot of **so called** experts all saying different things about diet.

Sara: Well, I reckon if you eat fresh food most of the time, you'll be **on the right track** and feeling great **in no time**. And it's important to read the labels on food too. Sometimes products are advertised as healthy but when you read the label they're full of sugar or salt.

Pam: Mm. I should start checking labels.

Sara: Well, there's a really great store in the main street. It sells all kinds of healthy food - fruit, **veggies**, healthy snacks - **you name it**. In fact, I'm heading down that way now. If you like, I'll show you.

Pam: OK. Well, you've inspired me! I'm going to **turn over a new leaf**.

Sara: And if you like you can come walking in the mornings.

Pam: Mm. Maybe. What time? …

Now let's see what these expressions mean - look at the next page.

CONVERSATION 2 (explanation of everyday expressions)

Compare Conversation 1 with Conversation 2 - You will see that some of the words are different but the meaning is the same in both conversations. Find the underlined words in Conversation 1, then underline the words with the same meaning in Conversation 2. Example: *Long time no see.* (Conversation 1) = *I haven't seen you for a long time.* (Conversation 2)

Sara: Hi Pam. <u>I haven't seen you for a long time</u>. How are you?

Pam: Hi Sara. Good to see you. You look great!

Sara: Thanks. I've been on a special health programme since the last time I saw you. You know - exercise program, special diet - all things relating to this.

Pam: A diet? But you didn't need to lose weight, did you?

Sara: I didn't really go on the diet to lose weight; it was about feeling better. Before the diet I was feeling really very tired. I didn't have any energy or excitement, or energy to do things. Now I'm feeling very well and happy. I've never felt better.

Pam: Well the effort has been successful. You look really great. And you mentioned exercise. Did you go to the gym?

Sara: Yeah, I exercised at the gym in the beginning and it helped me begin well. Now I go for a walk every morning before breakfast and it puts me in a good way of thinking for the rest of the day.

Pam: Wow. I should do something like that. Trouble is I don't have any will power with regard to food. I plan to eat only healthy food but then I see something very good to eat and my good plans are forgotten, don't happen.

Sara: I know. I've done that too. As the saying goes: 'It's difficult to change habits you've had for a long time'. But really it's a matter of changing your way of thinking, opinions about what's yummy.

Pam: I know I eat too much junk food and not enough green vegetables.

Sara: Well I've learnt that healthy food doesn't have to be boring – it can be yummy too.

Pam: I guess so. But I get confused when it comes to knowing what's best. There are a lot of incorrectly called experts all saying different things about diet.

Sara: Well, I reckon if you eat fresh food most of the time, you'll be doing the right thing for success and feeling great very soon. And it's important to read the labels on food too. Sometimes products are advertised as healthy but when you read the label they're full of sugar or salt.

Pam: Mm. I should start checking labels.

Sara: Well, there's a really great food store in the main street. It sells all kinds of healthy food - fruit, vegetables, healthy snacks - and many more things. In fact, I'm heading down that way now. If you like, I'll show you.

Pam: OK. Well, you've inspired me! I'm going to start doing things in a better way.

Sara: And if you like you can come walking in the mornings.

Pam: Mm. Maybe. What time? …

> Now to become familiar with the everyday expressions, practise CONVERSATION 1 aloud with a partner.

◄◄ **Replay Conversation 1**

Listen to the conversation again and write in the missing words. You may have to listen more than once. (Don't worry about your spelling as this exercise focuses on listening skills - you can check your spelling later.)

Sara: Hi Pam. _____ time no see. How are you?

Pam: Hi Sara. Good to see you. You look great!

Sara: Thanks. I've been on a <u>health</u> _____ since the last time I saw you. You know - exercise program, special diet – <u>the</u> _____.

Pam: A diet? But you didn't need to lose weight, did you?

Sara: I didn't really go on the diet to lose weight; it was about feeling better. Before the diet I was feeling really <u>burnt</u> _____. I didn't have any <u>oomph</u>, or <u>get up and</u> _____. Now I'm feeling <u>on</u> _____ of the world. I've never felt better.

Pam: Well the effort has <u>paid</u> ____. You look really great. And you mentioned exercise. Did you go to the gym?

Sara: Yeah, I <u>worked</u> _____ at the gym in the beginning and it <u>got me</u> _____ to a good start. Now I go for a walk every morning before breakfast and it puts me in <u>a good frame of</u> _____ for the rest of the day.

Pam: Wow. I should do something like that. Trouble is I don't have any will power <u>when it</u> _____ to food. I plan to eat only healthy food but then I see something <u>yummy</u> and my good plans <u>go out the</u> _____.

Sara: I know. I've done that too. As the saying goes: <u>'Old habits</u> _____ hard'. But really it's a matter of changing your <u>mind</u> _____ about what's yummy.

Pam: I know. I eat too much junk food and not enough_____.

Sara: Well I've learnt that healthy food doesn't have to be boring – it can be yummy too.

Pam: I guess so. But I get <u>bamboozled</u> when it comes to knowing what's best. There are a lot of_____ <u>called</u> experts all saying different things about diet.

Sara: Well. I reckon if you eat fresh food most of the time, you'll be <u>on the right</u> _____ and feeling great <u>in</u> _____ time. And it's important to read the labels on food too. Sometimes products are advertised as healthy but when you read the label they're full of sugar or salt.

Pam: Mm. I should start checking labels.

Sara: Well, there's a really great store in the main street. It sells all kinds of healthy food – fruit, <u>veggies</u>, healthy snacks – <u>you</u> _____ it. In fact I'm heading down that way now. If you like, I'll show you.

Pam: OK. Well, you've inspired me! I'm going to <u>turn over a new</u> _____.

Sara: And if you like you can come walking in the mornings.

Pam: Mm. Maybe. What time? …

> Now check your answers by comparing this page with CONVERSATION 1.

In order to become more familiar with these new everyday expressions:

◀◀ **Replay Conversation 1**

1) **Listen and tick the boxes** ☑ **next to the expressions as you hear them.**

2) **Write the definitions you can remember. (The first one has been done as an example.)**
   Check your answers with the reference list on page 126.

☐ Long time no see! ………………. <u>I haven't seen you for a long time!</u>

☐ * health kick…………………...…… _____

☐ the works …………………………… _____

☐ burnt out ……...………………..…… _____

☐ oomph. …………………………… _____

☐ get up and go ……………………… _____

☐ on top of the world……………….. _____

☐ paid off …………………………… _____

☐ worked out (at the gym)………….. _____

☐ got me off to a good start……….... _____

☐ * good frame of mind……………… _____

☐ when it comes to (something)…….. _____

☐ yummy……………………………… _____

☐ (plans) go out the window ……….. _____

☐ 'Old habits die hard' ……………… _____

☐ mindset …………………………… _____

☐ greens……………………………… _____

☐ bamboozled………………………… _____

☐ * so called (something)……………. _____

☐ on the right track………………….. _____

☐ in no time…………………………… _____

☐ veggies……………………………… _____

☐ you name it………………………… _____

☐ turn over a new leaf……………… _____

LANGUAGE NOTES

* Health kick' generally refers to a short term programme or activity, eg. He's on an exercise kick.

* The expression 'frame of mind' can also be expressed as 'state of mind'.

* The expression '<u>so-called</u>' is generally used before a noun phrase. We use 'so-called' before a word when we want to show we think the word is not correct or not suitable. For example:
   His *so-called good friends* didn't help him when he needed them. They are <u>not</u> really 'good friends'.

CROSSWORD - LANGUAGE REVIEW

Complete the sentences, choosing from the everyday expressions listed below. You can use the clues in brackets ( ) at the end of each sentence to help you. Then complete the crossword using the everyday expressions you have written. One has been done as an example.

so called	~~the works~~	go out the window	on top of the world	pay off
work out	frame of mind	in no time	you name it	turn over a new leaf

ACROSS

1) The college has a library, a canteen, a computer room, *the works*! (all things related to this situation)

3) This ___ _____ 'fruit juice' is just water, sugar and colouring. (incorrectly called)

5) If you don't save enough money, your plans will ___ _____ ____ _____. (not happen)

7) If you study well before the exam, it will _____ _____. (be successful)

9) I bought everything for the party – food, drink, glasses - _____ _____ __ (and many more things)

DOWN

2) Relaxation and enough sleep will improve your _____ ____ _____. (way of thinking)

4) After I started walking every day, I felt better ___ ____ _____. (very soon, quickly)

6) I'm going to _____ _____ __ ____ _____ and eat healthy food! (start doing things a better way)

8) Since I started exercising, I've felt ___ _____ ___ _____ _____. (very well and happy)

10) I'm going to _____ _____ at the gym twice a week. (exercise my body)

Check your answers on page 115.

FOCUS ON SPOKEN LANGUAGE

A) Prepositions such as 'on' and 'off'

Prepositions such as 'on' and 'off' can be used in various ways.
For example, in Conversation 1 (page 30) Sara says she's been 'on a health kick'.
 In this situation, '**on**' means to be involved in the <u>process of something happening</u>. eg. I'm <u>on</u> a diet.
  '**off**' means the <u>process finished, isn't happening or was cancelled</u>, eg. The trip is <u>off</u>.

Look at some examples:

on	off
I'm **on** a special programme. They're **on** vacation. He's **on** a long trip. I'm **on** a training course.	I'm **off** the diet now. (it's finished) The vacation is **off**. (not happening) The trip is **off**. (not happening) The training course is **off**. (cancelled)

Another way we use '**on**' and '**off**' is related to <u>using or operating equipment.</u>
Look at some examples:

on	off
She's **on** the phone. (using) He's **on** the computer. (using) I'll turn the light **on**. (operate) Turn the TV **on**, please.	She's **off** the phone now. (not using) He's **off** the computer. (not using) The light's are **off**. (not operating) Turn the TV **off** if you're not watching it.

There are many other ways 'on' and 'off' can be used. Look at the following examples from
Conversation 1.

Practice
There are several expression containing '**on**' and '**off**' used in Conversation 1.
Find them on page 30 and complete expressions below.

Now I'm feeling____ top of the world.   Well the effort has paid _____...

... you'll be_____ the right track...   It got me_____ to a good start...

B) Sequencing in storytelling

In English, we use different verb forms to show differences in time. The verb forms that show
time differences are called 'tenses'. For example, we talk about 'past tense', 'present tense', or
'future tense'.

In conversation, when we tell a story, it may involve the past, present and future but we don't
always start from the past and tell the story in the sequence that it happened. In fact, most
conversations, 'jump around' in time. In other words, the topic may start in the present, then go
to the past, then go to the future, then back to the past and finish in the future.

FOCUS ON SPOKEN LANGUAGE

B) Sequencing in storytelling (continued)

Look at the sentences from Conversation 1 in the table below.
They are in the time order or sequence they were spoken about, but <u>not</u> in the order they actually happened.

Read the sentences from Conversation 1 (on the left below) and decide when the action happened or will happen.

Write **past**, **present** or **future** or **past to present** or **present to future** next to each sentence. The first two sentences have been done as examples.

Sentences spoken by the speakers in Conversation 1	Past/present/future
1. You look great!	present
2. I've been on a health kick since the last time I saw you.	past to present
3. Before the diet I was feeling really burnt out.	
4. Now I'm feeling on top of the world	
5. You look really great.	
6. I worked out at the gym in the beginning and it got me off to a good start.	
7. Now I go for a walk every morning before breakfast	
8. I eat too much junk food and not enough greens	
9. But I get bamboozled when it comes to knowing what's best.	
10. I should start checking labels.	
11. I'm heading down that way now... I'll show you.	
12. Well, you've inspired me!	
13. I'm going to turn over a new leaf.	
14. And if you like you can come walking in the mornings.	

You can check the answers on page 116.

FOCUS ON SPOKEN LANGUAGE

C) As the saying goes:

A 'saying' is a short, well-known statement that expresses a meaning or idea that most people believe is true and wise. For example in Conversation 1 Sara says:

As the saying goes: Old habits die hard'.

Here are some more popular 'sayings'. What do you think they mean? Write the correct 'meanings' next to the appropriate 'saying'. You can check your answers on page 116.

'Sayings'   **Meanings**

1) 'Make hay while the sun shines.' _____

2) 'A problem shared is a problem halved.' _____

3) 'Practice makes perfect.' _____

4) 'Many hands make light work.' _____

5) 'The proof of the pudding is in the eating.' _____

6) 'Don't count your chickens before they're hatched.'_____

_____

Meanings – write the correct meaning next to the appropriate 'sayings' above.

a) Do something when you have the opportunity.

b) Don't make definite plans until you've seen how a particular situation develops.

c) It can help to talk about a problem with another person.

d) If many people help with something, the work will be easier.

e) Something can only be judged after it has been tried in a practical way.

f) Doing an activity many times makes you do the activity well.

Answers, page 116

FOCUS ON SPOKEN LANGUAGE

D) When it comes to …

The expression, '**when it comes to** (something)', is used twice in Conversation 1 and means 'with regard to (something)'. Check Conversation 1(page 30) and complete the sentences below.

1) Pam: …Trouble is _____ when it comes to _____.

2) Pam: I guess so. But _____when it comes to _____.

Answers, page 116.

We use 'when it comes to…', to talk about what we usually do in a particular situation
For example: 'When it comes to money, I usually spend more than I should.'

Complete these sentences about you:

When it comes to learning English, I usually_____.

When it comes to food, I usually_____.

It's a matter of…

The expression '**it's a matter of**' is used to say that getting a particular result involves doing a particular thing.

Check Conversation 1(page 30) and complete the sentences below.

3) Sara: But really _____ about what's yummy.

Answer, page 116.

Giving an opinion using: When it comes to … it's a matter of…

We can use both the expressions in the same sentence to give

our opinion about what should be done in a particular situation.

For example:
When it comes to losing weight, it's a matter of eating less food.
When it comes to getting enough sleep, it's a matter of going to bed by 10 pm.

Notice in the examples above that the …ing form of the verb is used in each part of the sentence.

Practice

Give your opinion by completing the following sentences.

When it comes to staying warm in winter, it's a matter of _____

When it comes to staying cool in summer, it's a matter of _____

When it comes to being happy, it's a matter of _____

When it comes to staying healthy, it's a matter of _____

E) Nouns used as adjectives

It is common in English to use nouns as adjectives by placing them before other nouns.
Some example are: junk food, exercise bike, breakfast cereal, fruit juice, food processor.
In the examples above, the first word *describes* the second word.

When nouns are put together in this way, they are sometimes written as one word; particularly if the words are short and commonly used.

Expressions such as these are often pronounced with the stress on the first word.

For example: <u>tea</u>spoon, <u>home</u>work, <u>track</u>suit, <u>tea</u>cup, <u>post</u>card, <u>pin</u>head.

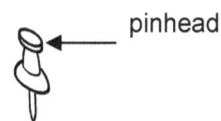

pinhead

If you are not sure where to put stress in a new word, your dictionary will help you.

Dictionaries use various symbols or marks to show which part of a word should be stressed, so it's important to check which symbol **your** dictionary uses.

For example, in the word '**pinhead**' (which has two syllables), the stress is on the first syllable. Look at the way this may be shown in a dictionary.

Some dictionaries show a stress mark **' before and above** the stressed syllable.   eg. /ˈpɪnhed/

Some dictionaries show a stress mark **' after and above** the stressed syllable.   eg. /pɪnˈhed/

Some dictionaries use **a line under** the stressed syllable, to show the stressed part. eg. /p<u>ɪn</u>hed/

To avoid confusion, always check which symbol **your** dictionary uses.

For more everyday expressions relating to 'health and sickness', see:
'Understanding Everyday Australian - Book 1', Unit 5, 'Visiting the Doctor'.

For more topics relating to 'health and medicine', see:
'Understanding English Pronunciation' - Unit 7 'Health and Happiness'
'Understanding English Pronunciation' - Unit 8 'Medical Miracles'

See final page of this book for details.

(Units 1 - 3)

This section reviews some of the expressions that were introduced in Units 1, 2, and 3 and gives you a chance to see what you have remembered.

Look at the pictures on the opposite page and decide what the people are saying by choosing from the expressions below.

Match each picture with an appropriate expression by writing the correct letter in the box next to each expression.

For extra practice, you could write the appropriate expression in the space provided in the picture.

1) When I see yummy food, my diet goes out the window. ☐

2) I've explained all the dos and don'ts, so if you study hard it will pay off. ☐

3) If you eat fresh food most of the time, you'll be in shape no time. ☐

4) They are getting on like a house on fire! ☐

5) Going to Asia was an eye opener for me. ☐

6) Oh no. I put my foot in it when I said she'd put on weight! ☐

7) When it comes to good food and drink, this cafe's got the works! ☐

8) I'm completely burnt out, Doctor. ☐

9) It's so good to unwind and just do my own thing. ☐

(Answers: page 117)

(Units 1 - 3)

UNIT 4

THE ENVIRONMENT

The term environment refers to 'the air, water and land where people, animals and plants live.'
Cambridge Learners Dictionary

Vietnam - Image courtesy of Vietnam CREB with provision courtesy of
Clean Up the World Ltd

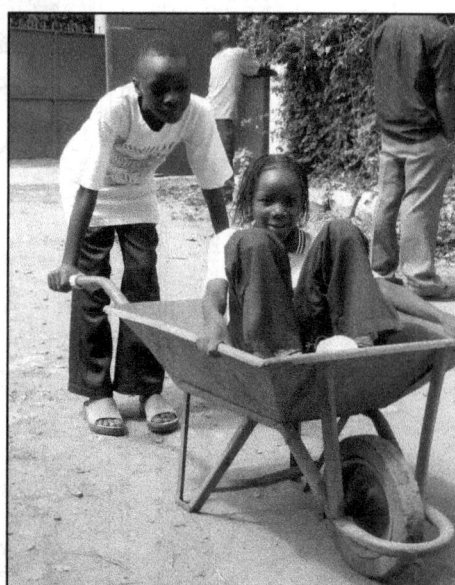

Kenya - Image courtesy of Jericho Arise with provision
courtesy of Clean Up the World Ltd

Mexico - Image courtesy of Pro Defence de Nazas with provision courtesy with
provision courtesy of Clean Up the World Ltd

India - Image courtesy of People Science Forum with
provision courtesy of Clean Up the World Ltd

In this unit you will listen to a conversation between friends who are talking about the environment. The conversation contains everyday expressions that will be explained later in the unit - so don't worry if you don't understand every word. This time you are listening for general understanding of the topic.

Part 1 - Pre Listening

Before listening, match the following words with the definitions below.

a campaign	a challenge	participate	responsibility	recycle

1. be involved with people in an activity_____   2. a difficult job or situation _____

3. a duty to do something _____   4. use something again _____

5. an organised activity for a special purpose _____

Listening for general understanding

Now listen to the conversation and tick the correct answers below:

1) What are the people in Julie's area cleaning this year?

a) the city beach

b) the local river

c) the local park

2) How many people helped in the Clean Up the World Campaign last year?

a) more than 30 million

b) more than 3 million

c) more than 1 million

3) Which of the following things does Julie suggest that Chris could do to help the environment?

a) use less electricity

b) plant some trees

c) use less water

Answers, page 117.

> Now, we'll look at the everyday expressions used in the conversation – turn to the next page.

CONVERSATION 1 (with everyday expressions)

◄◄ Replay Conversation 1
Read this conversation as you listen to the audio recording. Do you know what the _underlined_ words mean? They are colloquial or 'everyday' expressions.

Julie: I've **made up my mind** to join the Clean Up the World campaign this year. I'm excited!

Chris: What's that all about?

Julie: It's about people **getting together** to clean up their local environment. This year they're cleaning up the local river. You'd be surprised how much stuff, especially plastic, ends up in the river.

Chris: Mm. Sounds good but I think it's a waste of time. **There's no point** trying to **fix up** the environment.

Julie: What do you mean?

Chris: Well, your effort would be **a drop in the ocean**. Anyway **it's up to** the politicians to **take the lead** on these issues. **Our hands are tied**!

Julie: Well, I agree it's a challenge. But **when it comes to the crunch** the environment is **everyone's business**. That's why we all need to **pull together** and **get behind** the campaign. If we all **do our bit**, we can make a difference.

Chris: But a few people picking up plastic bags out of the river aren't going to save the world. **It'll take more than that**!

Julie: Well there are more than a few people **lending a hand**... I was just reading on the Clean Up the World website that more than 30 million people from all over the world **joined in** the campaign last year. You have to agree that's pretty good! And do you know how it started?

Chris: No, how?

Julie: One man, an Australian, Ian Kiernan saw the pollution in Sydney Harbour and decided to **take up** the challenge to clean it up. So he organised a community campaign and it was a great success. That led to the **setting up** of the Clean Up the World campaigns and now over a hundred countries **take part**.

Chris: OK **point taken**. But I don't want to get in the river.

Julie: Oh there are lots of ways you can get behind the campaign without even leaving your house!

Chris: **Such as**?

Julie: Well there's using less water, using less electricity, recycling plastic...

Now let's see what these expressions mean - look at the next page.

CONVERSATION 2 (explanation of everyday expressions)

Compare Conversation 1 with Conversation 2 -You will see that some of the words are different but the meaning is the same in both conversations. Find the underlined words in Conversation 1, then underline the words with the same meaning in Conversation 2. For example: made up my mind (Conversation 1) = decided (Conversation 2)

Julie: I've <u>decided</u> to join the Clean Up the World campaign this year. I'm excited!

Chris: What's that all about?

Julie: It's about people meeting to clean up their local environment. This year they're cleaning up the local river. You'd be surprised how much stuff, especially plastic, ends up in the river.

Chris: Mm. Sounds good but I think it's a waste of time. There's no good reason or purpose trying to repair or improve the environment.

Julie: What do you mean?

Chris: Well, your effort would be a very small amount; not enough for what is needed. Anyway it's the decision and responsibility of the politicians to be an example, lead on these issues. We don't have the power to do anything!

Julie: Well, I agree it's a challenge. But when the situation has become serious the environment is something everyone should know about. That's why we all need to co-operate and support the campaign. If we all help to do some work, we can make a difference.

Chris: But a few people picking up plastic bags out of the river aren't going to save the world. That will not be enough! It will require more.

Julie: Well there are more than a few people helping … I was just reading on the Clean Up the World web site that more than 30 million people from all over the world participated in the campaign last year. You have to agree that's pretty good! And do you know how it started?

Chris: No, how?

Julie: One man, an Australian, Ian Kiernan saw the pollution in Sydney Harbour and decided to begin the challenge to clean it up. So he organised a community campaign and it was a great success. That led to the beginning and preparing of the Clean Up the World campaigns and now over a hundred countries are involved, participate.

Chris: OK I understand your idea about this. But I don't want to get in the river.

Julie: Oh there are lots of ways you can get behind the campaign without even leaving your house!

Chris: What is an example?

Julie: Well there's using less water, using less electricity, recycling plastic...

> Now to become familiar with the everyday expressions, practise reading CONVERSATION 1 aloud with a partner.

◄◄ **Replay Conversation 1**

Listen to the conversation again and fill in the missing words. You may need to listen more than once. (Don't worry about your spelling as this activity focuses on listening skills; you can check your spelling later.)

Julie: I've <u>made up my</u>_____ to join the Clean Up the World campaign this year. I'm excited!

Chris: What's that all about?

Julie: It's about people <u>getting together</u> to clean up their local environment. This year they're cleaning up the local river. You'd be surprised how much stuff, especially plastic, ends up in the river.

Chris: Mm .Sounds good but I think it's a waste of time. <u>There's no</u>_____ trying to <u>fix</u>_____ the environment.

Julie: What do you mean?

Chris: Well, your effort would be <u>a</u>_____ <u>in the ocean</u>. Anyway <u>it's</u>_____ to the politicians to _____ <u>the lead</u> on these issues. <u>Our</u>_____ <u>are tied</u>!

Julie: Well, I agree it's a challenge. But <u>when it comes to the</u>_____ the environment is <u>everyone's business</u>. That's why we all need to _____ <u>together</u> and <u>get</u>_____ the campaign. If we all <u>do our</u>_____, we can make a difference.

Chris: But a few people picking up plastic bags out of the river aren't going to save the world. <u>It'll take more than that!</u>

Julie: Well there are more than a few people <u>lending a</u>_____... I was just reading on the Clean Up the World web site that more than 30 million people from all over the world <u>joined</u>_____the campaign last year. You have to agree that's pretty good! And do you know how it started?

Chris: No, how?

Julie: One man, an Australian, Ian Kiernan saw the pollution in Sydney Harbour and decided to <u>take up</u> the challenge to clean it up. So he organised a community campaign and it was a great success. That led to the <u>setting</u>_____ of the Clean Up the World campaigns and now over a hundred countries <u>take</u>_____.

Chris: OK _____ <u>taken</u>. But I don't want to get in the river.

Julie: Oh there are lots of ways you can get behind the campaign without even leaving your house!

Chris: <u>Such</u>_____?

Julie: Well there's using less water, using less electricity, recycling plastic...

> Now check your answers by comparing this page with CONVERSATION 1.

In order to become more familiar with these new everyday expressions:

◄◄ Replay Conversation 1

1) Listen and tick the boxes ☑ next to the expressions as you hear them.
2) Write the definitions you can remember. (The first one has been done as an example.)
   Check your answers with the reference list on page 127.

☐	made up my mind	_decided_ _____
☐	getting together...........................	_____
☐	There's no point........................	_____
☐	fix up	_____
☐	a drop in the ocean	_____
☐	it's up to (someone)....................	_____
☐	take the lead	_____
☐	Our hands are tied......................	_____
☐	when it comes to the crunch	_____
☐	everyone's business	_____
☐	pull together	_____
☐	get behind (the campaign)...........	_____
☐	do our bit.................................	_____
☐	It'll take more than that	_____
☐	lending a hand	_____
☐	joined in	_____
☐	take up	_____
☐	setting up	_____
☐	take part	_____
☐	point taken	_____
☐	Such as?	_____

LANGUAGE NOTE

*The expression '**a drop in the ocean**' can also be expressed as '**a drop in the bucket**'.
 These expressions have the same meaning.

* The expression '**take the lead**' can also be expressed as '**set the lead**'.

*In Conversation 1 of this unit the expression '**get behind**' the campaign means to give support.
 However, the expression '**get behind in**' an activity or '**get behind with**' an activity means to be
 slow, not making the expected progress in an activity.

   Remember, the meaning of an expression will depend on the context of the conversation.

CROSSWORD - LANGUAGE REVIEW

Complete the sentences, choosing from the everyday expressions listed below. You can use the clues in brackets ( ) at the end of each sentence to help you. Then complete the crossword using the everyday expressions you have written. One has been done as an example.

get behind	lend a hand	~~a drop in the ocean~~	do our bit	take the lead
pulled together	hands are tied	comes to the crunch	take part	fix up

ACROSS

1) The government provided money for the hospital improvements but it was _a drop in the ocean_. (a very small amount; not enough for what is needed)

3) If we want to get the job finished by Friday, we'll all have to ___ _____ _____(help do some work)

5) Don't move the heavy boxes by yourself! We'll all _____ ___ _____ later. (help)

7) Governments around the world should _____ _____ research into climate change. (support)

9) I think doctors should _____ _____ _____ in healthy living habits. (be an example)

DOWN

2) When it _____ ___ _____ _____, everyone will be affected by climate change. (when the situation becomes serious)

4) We can't do anything about the problem. Our _____ _____ _____. (we have no power)

6) When the storm ended, everyone _____ _____ to repair the damage. (co-operated)

8) When are you going to _____ ___ the garden. It looks very untidy! (repair, improve)

10) I'm going to _____ _____ in the campaign again this year. It was fun last year! (be involved)

Answers, page 117.

FOCUS ON SPOKEN LANGUAGE

A) The definite article

* 'the' is called the **definite article** because it can be used to talk about definite, specific, or unique things. For example, we use the definite article:

a) to talk about a specific place or thing because there is only one in the area.
   eg. We'll meet in **the** park.

b) when it is clear from the context which thing the speaker is taking about.
   eg. Could you put **the** flowers on **the** table please?

c) when we talk about things that have been mentioned previously in the conversation.
   eg. They planted trees there last year. You can see how big **the** trees have grown.

d) The definite article is also used when a thing or group of things is considered to be unique.
   Some examples are: **the** world, **the** sky, **the** sun, **the** moon, **the** stars, **the** equator, **the** earth.

e) The definite article is used before the titles of organisations and special events.
   For example: **the** World Health Organisation, **the** Royal Easter Show, **the** National Museum.

Pronunciation Note

The pronunciation of 'the' changes depending on the sound following it. When 'the' comes before a word with an initial vowel sound, as in, 'the earth', 'the' is pronounced with a long vowel sound, as in the word 'three'.

When 'the' comes before a word with an initial consonant sound as in, 'the world', 'the moon', it is pronounced with a weak, unstressed sound and shown in dictionaries by the symbol /ðə/.

Practice – The definite article

Find examples of the definite article in Conversation 1 (page 44) and complete the sentences below.

a) The definite article is used with a specific place or thing because there is only one in the area.
   'This year they're cleaning up_____.'

b) The definite article is used when it is clear from the context which thing the speaker is taking about.
   'But I don't want to get in _____.'

c) The definite article is used when something has been mentioned previously in the conversation.
   'Oh there are lots of ways to get behind _____.'

d) The definite article is used when a thing or group of things is considered to be unique.
   'But a few people picking up plastic bags out of the river aren't going to save _____.'

e) The definite article is used before the titles of organisations and special events.
   'I've made up my mind to join _____ this year.'

You can check your answers on page 117.

FOCUS ON SPOKEN LANGUAGE

Omission of the definite article

Generally, the definite article, 'the', isn't used before the names of people and places (but there are exceptions).

f) Find a sentence in Conversation 1 with examples of the name of a person and a place without 'the'. Answer, page 117.

'One man, an Australian, _____ saw the pollution in _____...

B) Uses of the word 'take'

The verb **'take'** is used in a variety of ways in English. Look at two examples from Conversation 1.

1) 'It'll take more than that!' In this context 'take' means 'require',
Another example: 'It'll take two of us to finish to the job today.'

2) 'OK point taken.' In this context 'taken' means 'understood' or 'accepted' something that was said.
Another example: 'I take your point.'

Find three more sentences with 'take' in Conversation 1. Complete the sentences below.

3) Anyway it's up to the politicians to_____

4) Ian Kiernan saw the pollution in Sydney Harbour and decided to _____

5) … now over a hundred countries _____. Answers, page 117

As an ordinary verb, 'take' can have a variety of meanings, depending on the context.

- 'take' can mean to do an action, eg. take a walk; take a breath; take a look; take a seat.

- 'take' can mean to carry with you, eg. It's raining so take your umbrella. Take these to the library.

- 'take' can mean to use transport, eg. take a bus; take a taxi; take a ride; take a train.

- 'take' can mean to remove something, eg. It will take the pain away. Take the cake from the box.

- 'take' can mean get something by using a machine, eg. take a photo; take an x-ray.

- 'take' can mean to accept something eg. take advice; take first prize; take a compliment.

- 'take' can mean study a subject, eg. take a computer course, take driving lessons.

- 'take' can mean need a particular amount of time, eg. It'll take twenty four hours to get to Spain.

- 'take' can mean require, eg. It will take a lot of effort to finish the course.

- 'take' can mean understand or accept something that was said, eg. Yes, I take your point.

- 'take' can mean remove without permission, eg. Don't take my wallet without asking me first!

- 'take' can mean consider as an example, eg. Most men like cars. Take my brother, he has two.

See phrasal verbs with 'take' on page 55.

C) Phrasal verbs

When a verb is followed by another word to form a particular meaning, this combination is called a 'phrasal verb'. Conversation 1 contains several phrasal verbs and expressions which mean to co-operate, to support or to participate and be involved. Check the meaning in Conversations 1 and 2, or check the Reference List (page 127) and write the most appropriate meaning next to each expression.

participate in	co-operate	support	be involved

1. 'pull together' _____   2. 'join in' _____

3. 'get behind' (an activity) _____   4. 'take part' _____

2. & 4. have a similar meaning

The answers are on page 118. You will find more information about phrasal verbs on page 54.

D) Describing what is happening

On pages 51 – 53 you will see pictures of people from around the world helping in the Clean Up the World campaigns.

Read the sentences below that describe what people are doing and what is happening in the pictures. The sentences use phrasal verbs and other expressions to describe what is happening.

When we describe something that is happening in a photo we can use the **ing** form of the verb.

Model sentences:

In China, the man and woman are **lending a hand** to collect rubbish.

The boys are **pulling together** to plant a tree.

The people are **taking part in** the Clean Up the World campaign.

The people are **getting behind** the campaign to clean up the beach.

The young boys are **doing their bit** to clean up the rubbish.

The men are **pulling together** to clear weeds from the river.

The people are **pulling together** to pull rubbish from the water.

The people are **joining in** the Clean Up the World campaign.

Practice

Write sentences for the photos on the following pages, describing what the people are doing.

Use the model sentences on this page or write your own sentences. The first one has been done as an example.

eg. **1)** _In Vietnam, the women are_

lending a hand to clear rubbish

from the river bank.

Vietnam - Image courtesy of CREB CUW with provision courtesy of Clean Up the World Ltd

Image courtesy of India - People Science Forum with provision courtesy of Clean Up the World Ltd

Write a sentence next to each photo, describing what the people are doing.

Use the model sentences on page 51 or write your own sentences.

2 _____

_____

_____

3 _____

_____

_____

Mexico - Image courtesy of Pro Defence de Nazas with provision courtesy of Clean Up the World Ltd

Mexico - Ajijic Limpio Beach clean up with provision courtesy of Clean Up the World Ltd

4 _____

_____

_____

5 _____

_____

_____

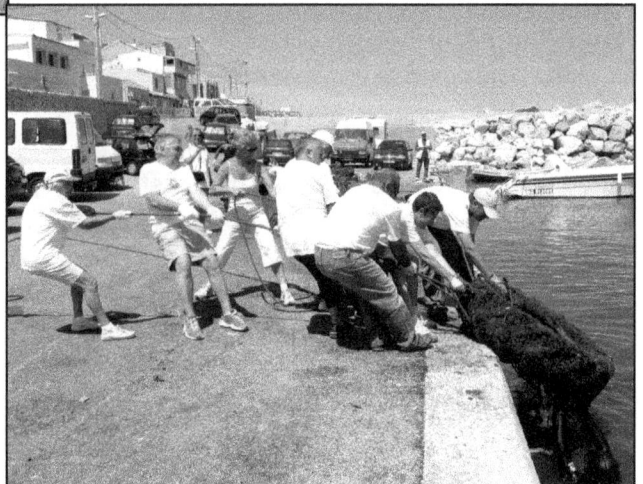

France Association Mer Terre with provision courtesy of Clean Up the World Ltd

South Africa DUCT Clean Up World Weekend provision courtesy of Clean Up the World Ltd

6 _____

_____

_____

7 _____

_____

_____

China- ShaoXing Bike Club provision courtesy of Clean Up the World Ltd

Papua New Guinea Ela Beah clean up Port Moresby - provision courtesy of Clean Up the World Ltd

8 _____

_____

_____

9 _____

_____

_____

Mexico Hayunlamiento do Zacapu provision courtesy of Clean Up the World Ltd

Reference page – Phrasal Verbs

When a verb is followed by one or two other words to form a particular meaning, this combination is called a '**phrasal verb**'. Phrasal verbs are very common in English; in fact there are thousands of 'phrasal verb' combinations used regularly in everyday English.

Some examples of phrasal verbs are: **go on** (means 'continue')
put up with (means 'endure')
runs out (means 'expires)
get out of (means '' avoid doing')

Phrasal verbs often cause problems for learners of English for the following reasons:

1) The individual meaning of the words are often different to the meaning of the words together in the 'phrasal verb' combination.

For example, students may understand the meaning of the word 'give' and the word 'up' but when they encounter the phrasal verb combination 'give up' (meaning 'quit') the meaning is not obvious without explanation.

2) Not all 'phrasal verbs' work the same way grammatically.
For example:
- When the object of the verb is a noun, the noun can go after the verb or in the middle of the phrasal verb,

         phrasal verb   object   object

    eg. Jane put on <u>her coat</u> or Jane put <u>her coat</u> on.

                                 phrasal verb

- When the object of the verb is replaced with a pronoun (it, her, him, we, they, etc), the pronoun goes in the middle of the phrasal verb.   object

                  eg. Jane put <u>it</u> on. (Not ~~Jane put on it~~.)

                    phrasal verb

    (Note: Some phrasal verbs can not be used with pronouns as objects.)

- Some commonly used phrasal verbs do not have objects.
Some examples are: I always <u>get up</u> early. When did he <u>get back</u>?
                          Please <u>go on</u>. She had to <u>get away</u>!

3) Particular phrasal verbs can have several meanings depending on the context.

For example: 'take off' can mean 'remove' as in: 'Take off your coat'.
               'take off' can mean 'leave the ground' as in: 'When will the plane take off?'

As there are many phrasal verbs commonly used in English, students should try to learn the meaning of each expression as it is encountered **in context**. As noted in the introduction, our choice of words is always dependent on the context or situation in which it is used. Therefore, when learning a new language, it is necessary to become familiar with the different contexts in which certain expressions are used before beginning to use them.

Reference page - Examples of phrasal verbs with the verb 'take'

taken aback means surprised, eg. 'He was **taken aback** by my expensive car.'

take after means to resemble a family member in appearance or habit, eg. I **take after** my mother.

take along something (or someone) means to have with you, eg. I always **take along** a notebook.

take away means to remove something, eg. The council came to **take away** the rubbish.

take back means return something borrowed or bought, eg. I'll **take back** the library books today.

take back means to admit you were wrong to say something, eg. I'm sorry. I **take back** that remark.

take down means write or record something, eg. I'll **take down** your address and phone number.

take down means remove from a high place, eg. Please **take down** the pictures and paint the wall.

take in (something you hear, read) means to understand, eg. Did you **take in** everything I said?

Note: If the police **take someone in** it means take to the police station. eg, 'We'll **take** him **in** for questioning'.

take off means to remove, eg. **Take off** your coat. Why don't you **take off** your wet shoes?

take off (in a plane) means to leave the ground. eg. What time does the plane **take off**?

take on (something) means to accept and try to do. eg. 'He'll **take on** the job of national manager.'

take on (someone) means start to employ, eg. The company will **take on** new staff this year.

take on (someone) means compete with, eg. England will **take on** Australia for the Ashes.

take out means to withdraw. eg. How much do we need to **take out** of our account?

take (someone) **out** means invite as a guest, eg. I'm **taking** her **out** to a special restaurant.

take over means to gain control, eg. A large company will **take over** our business next week.

take through means to show or discuss a task. eg. I'll **take** you **through** the timetable.

take to (something or someone) means to like, eg. I couldn't **take to** him.

take up (an activity) means begin to do, eg. I'm going to **take up** fishing when I retire.

take (someone) **up on** something means to accept an offer, eg. I'll **take** you **up on** your offer.

taken with (something) means impressed or pleased by it. eg. I'm very **taken with** his idea.

This is not a complete list. For a complete list of phrasal verbs with 'take' check your dictionary
or a book specifically about 'phrasal verbs'.

UNIT 5

FEARS AND PHOBIAS

The topic you will hear discussed in this unit is about the phobias or fears that people have of everyday things such as storms, flying, heights or going in a lift.

A phobia is described as 'a very strong feeling of disliking or being afraid of someone or something'. Macmillan English Dictionary for Advanced Learners, 2002 edition

A phobia is described as 'an extreme fear of something' in the Cambridge Learner's Dictionary, 2003

Part 1 - Pre Listening

In this unit you will listen to a conversation between friends who are talking about fears and phobias. Before you listen to the conversation, look at the illustrations on the previous page. Which of the following words describe the phobia in each illustration? Write the correct number next to each description below. (Answers, page 118)

storms ___   heights ___   insects___   going in a lift ___   flying ___   mice ___

Before listening, match each word to its correct meaning below. Answers, page 118.

thunder   scared   a lift   high-rise   stuck   avoid

1. afraid _____   2. an elevator _____   3. a loud noise in the sky _____

4. a building with many levels _____   5. stay away from _____   6. trapped _____

Listening for general understanding

The conversation contains colloquial expressions that will be explained later in the unit, so don't worry if you don't understand every word. This time you are listening for general understanding of the topic. As you listen, tick the correct answers below, then check your answers on page 118.

1) Don doesn't want to go to the restaurant with Kara
   because he's afraid of:

   a) flying

   b) going in lifts

2) Kara has a phobia about :

   a) spiders

   b) mice

   c) cats

3) Kara's brother is scared of:

   a) storms

   b) dogs

Answers, page 118.

Now we'll look at the everyday expressions used in the conversation – turn to the next page.

CONVERSATION 1 (with everyday expressions)

◀◀ Replay Conversation 1
Read this conversation as you listen to the audio recording. Do you know what the
underlined **words mean? They are colloquial or everyday expressions.**

Kara: Hey Don. We're all going to the new Skyline restaurant for our end of year **get-together**. Can we **count you in**? It's on the 28th floor and it has amazing views of the city!

Don: Oh thanks Kara but **I'll pass** this time.

Kara: Oh Don, are you sure you can't make it? We don't get together very often.

Don: Look I'll **come clean** with you Kara – I **have a thing about** lifts so I don't want to go to dinner on the 28th floor.

Kara: A thing about lifts? But I've seen you go in lifts.

Don: Yes, but only if I'm with someone and don't want to **lose face**, or if I can't **get out of it** - like in a high-rise hotel where you have to use a lift. Then I just **grin and bear it** and **hold my breath** until the doors open and I'm back on the ground floor. I know it's stupid; I've never been stuck in a lift - **touch wood**!

Kara: Oh don't worry about it Don. I think most people have a phobia about something. **Take** my boss - she's got a thing about **creepy crawlies** and I'm **scared stiff** of mice – even tiny ones! I **freaked out** last week when I **found out** there was a mouse in the office. And yet the lady I work with wasn't **fazed** at all. It was very funny really. I was standing on a chair! We had a good laugh about it later.

Don: Yeah it helps to **have a sense of humour**. We have to laugh at ourselves.

Kara: Absolutely. My brother is scared stiff of storms. He **jumps out of his skin** every time there's loud thunder. He's **working on it** though because he doesn't want it to **get the better of him**.

Don: Mm. I guess most phobias can be **mind over matter**. It's like my lift phobia; I don't **let it get out of hand**.

Kara: Does that mean you'll come to the restaurant?

Don: Only if I can bring my pet mouse with me!

| Now let's see what these expressions mean - look at the next page. |

CONVERSATION 2 (explanation of everyday expressions)

Compare Conversation 1 with Conversation 2 -You will see that some of the words are different but the meaning is the same in both conversations. Find the underlined words in Conversation 1, then underline the words with the same meaning in Conversation 2.
For example: _get-together_ (Conversation 1) = _informal social meeting_ (Conversation 2)

Kara: Hey Don. We're all going to the new Skyline restaurant for our end of year informal meeting with friends. Can we include you? It's on the 28th floor and it has amazing views of the city!

Don: Oh, thanks Kara but I'll say 'no', not accept (the invitation) this time.

Kara: Oh Don, are you sure you can't make it? We don't get together very often.

Don: Look I'll be honest with you Kara – I have a dislike of (going in) lifts so I don't want to go to dinner on the 28th floor.

Kara: A thing about lifts? But I've seen you go in lifts.

Don: Yes, but only if I'm with someone and don't want to look foolish, or if I can't avoid doing it- like in a high-rise hotel where you have to use a lift. Then I just do it even if I don't want to and wait nervously until the doors open and I'm back on the ground floor. I know it's stupid; I've never been stuck in a lift - and I hope that good situation continues!

Kara: Oh don't worry about it Don. I think most people have a phobia about something. Take as an example (of this) my boss - she's got a thing about insects and I'm very afraid of mice - even tiny ones! I acted strangely because I was afraid last week when I learnt there was a mouse in the office. And yet the lady I work with wasn't worried at all. It was very funny really. I was standing on a chair! We had a good laugh about it later.

Don: Yeah it helps to be able to see funny situations in everyday life. We have to laugh at ourselves.

Kara: Absolutely. My brother is scared stiff of storms. He gets a sudden bad shock every time there's loud thunder. He's trying to improve the situation though because he doesn't want it to control him.

Don: Mm. I guess most phobias can be the power of your thoughts affecting how you feel about something. It's like my lift phobia; I don't let the situation get out of control.

Kara: Does that mean you'll come to the restaurant?

Don: Only if I can bring my pet mouse with me!

Now to become familiar with the everyday expressions, practise reading CONVERSATION 1 aloud with a partner.

◀◀ **Replay Conversation 1**

Listen to the conversation again and fill in the missing words. You may need to listen more than once. (Don't worry about your spelling as this activity focuses on listening skills; you can check your spelling later.)

Kara: Hey Don. We're all going to the new Skyline restaurant for our end of year <u>get-together</u>. Can we_____you in? It's on the 28th floor and it has amazing views of the city!

Don: Oh, thanks Kara but <u>I'll_____</u> this time.

Kara: Oh Don, are you sure you can't make it? We don't get together very often.

Don: Look I'll <u>come_____</u>with you Kara – I <u>have a_____</u> about lifts so I don't want to go to dinner on the 28th floor.

Kara: A thing about lifts? But I've seen you go in lifts.

Don: Yes, but only if I'm with someone and don't want to <u>lose_____</u>, or if I can't <u>get out of____</u> - like in a high-rise hotel where you have to use a lift. Then I just _____and bear it and _____<u>my breath</u> until the doors open and I'm back on the ground floor. I know it's stupid; I've never been stuck in a lift - <u>touch_____</u>!

Kara: Oh don't worry about it Don. I think most people have a phobia about something. <u>Take</u> my boss – she's got a thing about _____<u>crawlies</u> and I'm <u>scared_____</u> of mice - even tiny ones! I <u>freaked____</u> last week when I <u>found_____</u> there was a mouse in the office. And yet the lady I work with wasn't <u>fazed</u> at all. It was very funny really. I was standing on a chair! We had a good laugh about it later.

Don: Yeah it helps to <u>have a_____of humour</u>. We have to laugh at ourselves.

Kara: Absolutely. My brother is scared stiff of storms. He <u>jumps out of his_____</u> every time there's loud thunder. He's <u>working_____</u>it though because he doesn't want it to <u>get the_____of him</u>.

Don: Mm. I guess most phobias can be _____<u>over matter</u>. It's like my lift phobia; I don't <u>let it get out of_____</u>.

Kara: Does that mean you'll come to the restaurant?

Don: Only if I can bring my pet mouse with me!

Now check your answers by comparing this page with
CONVERSATION 1.

In order to become more familiar with these new everyday expressions:

◄◄ Replay Conversation 1

1) Listen and tick the boxes ☑ next to the expressions as you hear them.
2) Write the definitions you can remember. (Some have been done for you as examples.)
3) Check your answers by turning to page 128.

☐	get-together..............................	*informal meeting with friends* _____
☐	count you in...........................	_____
☐	I'll pass	_____
☐	come clean (about something)...	_____
☐	have a thing about (something)*	_____
☐	lose face*	_____
☐	get out of (doing something).......	_____
☐	grin and bear it	_____
☐	hold my breath	_____
☐	touch wood*	_____
☐	take (something or someone)	_____
☐	creepy crawlies........................	_____
☐	scared stiff	_____
☐	freaked out	_____
☐	found out.............................	_____
☐	wasn't fazed	_____
☐	have a sense of humour	_____
☐	jumps out of his skin................	_____
☐	working on it..........................	_____
☐	(not) let it get the better of you....	_____
☐	mind over matter....................	_____
☐	don't let it get out of hand..........	_____

LANGUAGE NOTES

* The expression, '*I have a thing about (something)*' can mean *I really <u>dislike</u> (something).*
However, depending on the context of the conversation, it can also mean, '*I really <u>like</u> (something).*'
eg. *He has a thing about motorbikes; he has several of his own. = He really likes motorbikes.*

* The expression '**lose face**' means to look foolish. The expression, to '**save face**' means to
do something so that you don't look foolish, eg. Despite his fear, he went in the lift to save face.

* When people say '**touch wood**' they often try to touch something made of wood with their hand.

* The expression 'Take my boss...' means 'My boss is an example of this...'.
See page 55 for more examples of uses of the word 'take'.

CROSSWORD - LANGUAGE REVIEW

Complete the sentences, choosing from the everyday expressions listed below. You can use the clues in brackets ( ) at the end of each sentence to help you. Complete the crossword using the everyday expressions you have written. The first one has been done as an example.
You can check your answers on page 118.

scared stiff	~~creepy crawlies~~	have a thing about	lose face
come clean	out of hand	Touch wood.	
freak out	jump out of my skin	grin and bear it	work on it

ACROSS

1) There are a lot of _creepy crawlies_ in the Australian bush. (insects)

3) I'm afraid of flying but I'm going overseas next year so I'll have to _____ ___ ___. (try to improve)

5) Did you hear the loud thunder. It made me _____ _____ ___ ___ _____.(get a sudden shock)

7) If you're afraid of your neighbour's dog, you should _____ _____ and tell her. (be honest)

9) I don't want to work in a high-rise. I _____ __ _____ _____heights. (have a dislike of)

11) I've never lost any money. _____ _____! (I hope the good situation continues.)

DOWN

2) I'm _____ _____ of spiders and snakes! (very afraid)

4) I _____ _____ if I see a mouse in the house. (act strangely because I'm afraid)

6) I hate going in lifts but I just _____ _____ _____ ___. (do it even when I don't want to)

8) I don't talk about my phobia because I don't want to _____ _____. (look foolish)

10) If a phobia gets _____ ___ _____ it can make your life very difficult. (out of control)

Answers, page 118.

FOCUS ON SPOKEN LANGUAGE

A) Word Linking in Spoken English

In fluent spoken English, words in a sentence are not all heard as separate words. Some words are linked together. This is referred to as 'connected speech'.

◄◄ **Replay the first line from Conversation. Listen to the *linking of words* in the following sentence.**

The linked sounds are shown with the symbol ‿ in between the linked words.

> Hey Don. We're‿all going to the new Skyline restaurant for‿our‿end‿of year get‿together.

Did you notice where words are linked together?

Examples of Word Linking

* Words that *end in a consonant sound* are linked to words that *begin with a vowel sound*

  For example: We're‿all... ...for‿our‿end‿of...

* Words that end with a *consonant sound* are linked to words *that begin with the same sound*.

  For example, the 't' sound in get‿together is linked. The linking sound is usually pronounced only *once*, but a little longer than usual.

Practice

Look at this sentence from Conversation 1.

> My brother is scared stiff of storms.
>
> He jumps out of his skin.

Mark ‿ where you think the speaker would link words in fluent speech.

You can check your answer on page 119.

See page 65 for more information and examples of connected speech.

B) Word combinations – using the correct preposition

When learning English it is useful to learn groups of words that always go together, rather than learning words in isolation. The word 'collocation' describes the way certain words combine in a language in natural speech. In English, particular prepositions (words such as, 'on', 'in', 'of', 'about') must be used in particular expressions in order to sound natural.

For example, in the sentence, 'Don't worry <u>about</u> it', the preposition 'about' is the only appropriate preposition to use after 'worry' in this sentence.

The following sentences have been taken from Conversation 1. Add the appropriate preposition to each sentence. You can use the words more than once. The answers are on page 119.

on	out	of	about	in

I think most people have a phobia _____ something. Take my boss - she's got a thing _____ creepy crawlies and I'm scared stiff _____ mice – even tiny ones! I freaked _____ last week when I found out there was a mouse ____ the office. I was standing _____ a chair! We had a good laugh _____ it later.

My brother is scared stiff_____ storms. He jumps _____ of his skin every time there's loud thunder. He's working _____ it though because he doesn't want it to get the better _____ him.

FOCUS ON SPOKEN LANGUAGE

C) Plural nouns

When we generalise about a fear or phobia we use the plural form of the noun. eg. mice, heights.

Using plural nouns, complete the sentences: Kara is scared of _____

Don has a thing about _____

Kara's brother is afraid of _____

An exception to this is when we use a word ending with 'ing'. For example: I'm afraid of flying.

D) Uses of 'only'

Many words in English have different meanings in different situations.
The word 'only' has several meanings. For example:

- only can mean 'not more than a particular number', eg. There are only three cakes left.
- only can mean 'not important or significant', eg. It's only a temporary job.
- only can mean 'limited to a particular person or thing', eg. 'Only the manager can do that.'

- The expression '**only if**...' is used to say that one condition or action is necessary for another thing to happen. For example: I'll go, but <u>only if</u> you go too.

He'll <u>only</u> know your address <u>if</u> you tell him.

Find two examples of 'only if...', spoken by Don, in Conversation 1.

1._____

2._____

Answers, page 119

Note:

The expression, '**If only**...' is different to the expression 'only if...' which is discussed above.

'If only...' is used to express a strong wish. For example:

'<u>If only</u> he would call me!' means '<u>I wish</u> he would call me!'

E) Synonyms

Synonyms are words that have a similar meaning to another word. Write the adjectives in the box next to their synonyms below. One has been done as an example.

frightened	glad	concerned	ashamed
~~brave~~	awful	foolish	amusing

unafraid	*brave* _____	scared	_____
stupid	_____	embarrassed	_____
worried	_____	terrible	_____
pleased	_____	funny	_____

Answers, page 119

Reference page - Understanding Connected Speech

When speaking in a natural, fluent, conversational way English speakers (including educated speakers) contract and link words to help the smooth flow of speech.
Words can be linked in the following ways:

1) A contracted word is linked to the word before it. An apostrophe (') is used to show where letters in the word have been left out.

   e.g. <u>We are</u> all going to the new restaurant . ——▶ <u>We're</u> all going to the new restaurant.
   Thanks but <u>I will</u> pass this time. ——▶ Thanks but <u>I'll</u> pass this time.
   <u>It is</u> on the 28th floor. ——▶ <u>It's</u> on the 28th floor.
   <u>We are</u> going fishing this weekend. ——▶ We're going fishing this weekend.

2) Unstressed words (called weak forms) are reduced. This means they are spoken quickly. For example, words like 'a', 'an', 'at', 'of', 'for', are often reduced in conversational speech.

   The unstressed <u>sound</u> is shown in the dictionary with the symbol / ə /.

   /ə/　　/ə/　　　　/ə/　　/ə/
   It helps to have a sense of humour. We have to laugh at ourselves.

   See Unit 1, Part 6A for more information on contractions and weak forms.

3) Words ending with a <u>consonant</u> sound and followed by words starting with a <u>vowel</u> sound are usually linked, eg. loo<u>k‿</u>out　　ope<u>n‿</u>up　　com<u>e‿</u>in ('e' in 'come' is silent)

4) Words ending with a <u>consonant sound</u> are generally linked to words starting with the <u>same consonant sound</u>. The sound is pronounced only once, but a little longer.

   e.g. We're having a get‿together.　　I'm at the bus‿stop. I'm having a good‿day.

5) In fast, connected speech some sounds may be deleted.
   For example, the sounds /d/ and /h/ are often deleted in unstressed words.
   /əv/　　　　　　　　　/ən/
   e.g. Some books h̶ave been written about fears an̶d phobias.

   In some groups of words such as '*going to*' and '*want to*', sounds are often deleted in fast speech. For example:　'going to' becomes 'gonna'
   'want to' becomes 'wanna'

   　　　　gonna　　　　　　　　　wanna
   e.g. We're going to have a party. Do you want to come?

6) Words ending with a <u>vowel</u> sound which are followed by words starting with a <u>vowel</u> sound can be linked with a 'linking sound'. For example, when words such as 'you' are followed by a word beginning with a vowel sound, speakers link the two words with the sound /w/, e.g. 'Can we count you‿in?'　'You‿are clever.'　Who‿else is going?
   　　　　　　　　　　　　　　　　　/w/　　　　/w/　　　　　　/w/

Note: It is not necessary for learners of English to link words in this way *to be understood* by others. However, it is important for students to be *aware* of these features of spoken English in order *to understand* the connected speech of English speakers and to realise that the use of these features helps the smooth flow of speech.

You can learn more about the pronunciation of English in the book and CD,
'Understanding English Pronunciation – an integrated practice course'.
See details on the final page of this book.

UNIT 6

PEOPLE AND RELATIONSHIPS

The term 'relationship' refers to the way people or groups of people feel and behave towards each other. We have different kinds of relationships with our family, friends and work colleagues, etc.

Part 1 - Pre Listening - Discussion

Do you agree or disagree with the following statements about people and relationships?

Good friendships and relationships always need time to develop.
People usually know immediately, the first time they meet, if they are going to be good friends.
People don't always like each other the first time they meet, but may later become good friends.

In this unit you will listen to a conversation between friends who are talking about another person. Kim is telling her friend, Pina, about what happened at work.

Listening for general understanding

The conversation contains colloquial expressions that will be explained later in the unit, so don't worry if you don't understand every word. This time you are listening for general understanding of the topic. As you listen, tick the correct answers below.
You can check your answers on page 119.

1) At the beginning of the conversation, Kim says,

a) her boss kept checking on her

b) her boss doesn't talk to her.

2) When Kim went to her bosses' office

a) he was angry and said,
'I'm too busy to see you.'

b) he was friendly and said,
'Oh I wanted to see you.'

3) When Kim's boss asked her to go out with him, Kim said,

a) 'OK. That would be nice.'

b) 'No, sorry.'

Now we'll look at the everyday expressions used in the conversation – turn to the next page.

CONVERSATION 1 (with everyday expressions)

◀◀ Replay Conversation 1

Read this conversation as you listen to the audio recording. Do you know what the _underlined_ words mean? They are colloquial or 'everyday' expressions.

Kim: Pina, you'll never guess what's happened!

Pina: Oh Kim. What?

Kim: Well, as you know, I've **had a lot on my plate** lately with my job. It's been so busy.

Pina: Yes, and I know you've been **on edge** because you don't **get on with** your boss.

Kim: Well **from the word go** I **bent over backwards** trying to do a good job. But he just kept checking on me all the time, **keeping tabs on** me. And we just **don't see eye to eye** about a lot of things.

Pina: You **spat the dummy** one day, didn't you? I remember you were really upset.

Kim: I wanted to but I didn't. I thought better of it and I **bit my tongue**. But I thought he was such **a show-off**; and always so **full of himself**!

Pina: **Come on, get on with** the story!

Kim: Sorry. Anyway today I thought, '**That's it**! I have to **get this off my chest**.' So I went to his office to **have it out** with him. And **to cut a long story short**, he said: 'Oh I wanted to see you', and he **was all smiles** which completely **caught me off guard**.

Pina: I can imagine.

Kim: He said he was very **taken with** my work and that I'd been such **a good sport** through a very busy time. And...wait for **the punch line**! He **asked me out**!

Pina: Oh, **you're pulling my leg**!

Kim: No.... I'm serious. I was **lost for words**.

Pina: And ....?

Kim: Well, I said, 'OK. That'd be nice'.

Pina: Well, You've **changed your tune**!

Kim: Yes, I know but......

> _I thought he was such a show off and so full of himself._

Now let's see what these expressions mean - look at the next page.

CONVERSATION 2 (explanation of everyday expressions)

Compare Conversation 1 with Conversation 2 - You will see that some of the words are different but the meaning is the same in both conversations. Find the underlined expressions in Conversation 1, then underline the words with the same meaning in Conversation 2.
For example: <u>had a lot on my plate</u> (Conversation 1) = <u>had a lot of work to do</u> (Conversation 2)

Kim: Pina, you'll never guess what's happened!

Pina: Oh Kim. What?

Kim: Well, as you know, I've <u>had a lot of work to do</u> lately with my job. It's been so busy.

Pina: Yes, and I know you've been nervous/not relaxed because you don't have a good relationship with your boss.

Kim: Well from the beginning I tried very hard to please (my boss) trying to do a good job. But he just kept checking on me all the time, watching me (and what I was doing). And we just don't agree about a lot of things.

Pina: You spoke angrily one day, didn't you? I remember you were really upset.

Kim: I wanted to but I didn't. I thought better of it and I didn't say anything although I wanted to. But I thought he was such a person who tells others he is very good and always so pleased with himself and thinks he is so important!

Pina: Hurry, continue with the story!

Kim: Sorry. Anyway today I thought, 'I'm going to deal with this situation! I have to talk about this problem.' So I went to his office to talk openly about it with him. And to tell you only the main part of the story, he said: 'Oh I wanted to see you', and he looked very friendly which completely surprised me.

Pina: I can imagine.

Kim: He said he was very pleased and impressed with my work and that I'd been such a pleasant person who didn't complain through a very busy time. And…wait for the last part of the story that makes it interesting! He invited me to go out somewhere with him.

Pina: Oh, you're telling me something that is not true!

Kim: No…. I'm serious. I was unsure what to say.

Pina: And ….?

Kim: Well, I said, 'OK. That'd be nice'.

Pina: Well, You've changed your opinion.

Kim: Yes, I know but……

Now to become familiar with the everyday expressions, practise reading CONVERSATION 1 aloud with a partner.

◀◀ **Replay Conversation 1**

Listen to the conversation again and fill in the missing words. You may need to listen more than once. (Don't worry about your spelling as this activity focuses on listening skills; you can check your spelling later.)

Kim: Pina, you'll never guess what's happened!

Pina: Oh Kim. What?

Kim: Well, as you know, I've <u>had a lot on my</u> _____ lately with my job. It's been so busy.

Pina: Yes, and I know you've been <u>on edge</u> because you don't _____ <u>on with</u> your boss.

Kim: Well <u>from the word</u> _____ I <u>bent</u> _____ <u>backwards</u> trying to do a good job. But he just kept checking on me all the time, <u>keeping tabs</u> _____ me. And we just <u>don't see</u> _____ <u>to eye</u> about a lot of things.

Pina: You _____ <u>the dummy</u> one day, didn't you? I remember you were really upset.

Kim: I wanted to but I didn't. I thought better of it and I _____ <u>my tongue</u>. But I thought he was such <u>a</u> _____ <u>-off</u>; and always so _____ <u>of himself</u>!

Pina: <u>Come on, get</u> _____ <u>with</u> the story.

Kim: Sorry. Anyway today I thought, '<u>That's it</u>! I have to <u>get this off my</u> _____.' So I went to his office to <u>have it</u> _____ with him. And <u>to</u> _____ <u>a long story short</u>, he said: 'Oh I wanted to see you', and he <u>was all</u> _____ which completely <u>caught me</u> _____ <u>guard</u>.

Pina: I can imagine.

Kim: He said he was very <u>taken with</u> my work and that I'd been such <u>a good</u> _____ through a very busy time. And...wait for <u>the</u> _____ <u>line</u>! He <u>asked me out</u>!

Pina: Oh, <u>you're pulling my</u> _____!

Kim: No.... I'm serious. I was _____ <u>for words</u>.

Pina: And ....?

Kim: Well, I said, 'OK. That'd be nice'.

Pina: Well, You've <u>changed your</u> _____!

Kim: Yes, I know but......

Now check your answers by comparing this page with
CONVERSATION 1.

In order to become more familiar with these new everyday expressions:

◄◄ Replay Conversation 1

1) Listen and tick the boxes ☐✓ next to the expressions as you hear them.

2) Write the definitions you can remember. (The first one has been done as an example.)
   Check your answers with the reference list on page 129.

☐ had a lot on my plate*............   *had a lot of work to do*

☐ on edge.................................   _____

☐ get on with.........................   _____

☐ from the word go ....   _____

☐ bent over backwards ....   _____

☐ keeping tabs on (me) ....   _____

☐ don't see eye to eye...............   _____

☐ spat the dummy ....   _____

☐ bit my tongue........................   _____

☐ a show-off ....   _____

☐ full of himself ....   _____

☐ Come on, get on with (something)*   _____

☐ That's it! ....   _____

☐ get this off my chest............   _____

☐ have it out..........................   _____

☐ to cut a long story short ....   _____

☐ all smiles...........................   _____

☐ caught me off guard ....   _____

☐ taken with (someone or something)   _____

☐ a good sport.......................   _____

☐ the punch line.....................   _____

☐ asked me out......................   _____

☐ you're pulling my leg............   _____

☐ lost for words......................   _____

☐ changed your tune..............   _____

LANGUAGE NOTE

* The expression, 'bent over <u>backwards</u>', can also be expressed as 'bent over <u>backward</u>'.

* 'get on with' is a phrasal verb that can have different meanings depending on the context.
In Conversation 1 'get on with' has been used twice, with different meanings.

For example, to 'not get on with' (someone) can mean 'not have a good relationship with them',
eg. 'You don't <u>get on with</u> your boss.' = 'You don't <u>have a good relationship</u> with your boss.'

Alternatively, 'get on with' (an activity) can mean 'continue doing it',
eg. '....<u>get on with</u> the story.' = '<u>continue telling</u> the story.'

CROSSWORD - LANGUAGE REVIEW

Complete the sentences, choosing from the everyday expressions listed below. You can use the clues in brackets ( ) at the end of each sentence to help you. Complete the crossword using the everyday expressions you have written. The first one has been done as an example.

off my chest	see eye to eye	have it out	change your tune
a show-off	the punch line	spat the dummy	full of herself
all smiles	a good sport	cut a long story short	

ACROSS

1) I'm upset and I have to get something *off my chest*. (talk about a problem)

3) He told some lies and I want to _____ ___ _____ with him. (talk openly about the problem)

5) He's very helpful and he's __ _____ _____. (a pleasant person who doesn't complain)

7) My mother-in-law and I don't _____ _____ __ _____ about the children. (agree)

9) I'm in a hurry so I'll _____ _ _____ _____ _____ ... (tell you only the main part of the story)

11) I don't like her. She is so _____ ___ _____. (thinks herself to be very important)

DOWN

2) When we met at the airport, she was ____ _____. (looked very friendly and happy)

4) You agreed with the plan. You can't _____ _____ _____ now! (change your opinion)

6) We were all surprised by _____ _____ _____ of his story. (the last part of the story that makes it interesting)

8) She was angry about the price so she _____ _____ _____. (spoke angrily)

10) I think he's ___ _____ _____ . He is always talking about what he can do. (a person who tells others he is very good)

Answers, page 119.

FOCUS ON SPOKEN LANGUAGE

A) Regular and irregular past tense verbs - review

To make the past tense, we add 'ed' to many verbs; we add 'd' when a word ends with 'e'.

ask ⟶ ask<u>ed</u>   want ⟶ want<u>ed</u>   save ⟶ save<u>d</u>   smile ⟶ smile<u>d</u>

Pronunciation of 'ed' endings

The 'ed' endings of words are pronounced as /t/, /d/, or /əd/ depending on the sound before 'ed'.

As a general rule:

- The 'ed' ending is pronounced as /t/ sound after soft consonant sounds such as: s, p, t, th, ch, k, sh.

  eg. kick<u>ed</u> is pronounced as /kɪkt/ (one syllable); miss<u>ed</u> is pronounced as /mɪst/ (one syllable)

- The 'ed' ending is pronounced as an extra syllable, /əd/, when added to words ending in /d/ or /t/.

  eg. When 'ed' is added to the word en<u>d</u> (1 syllable), end<u>ed</u> is pronounced as end<u>əd</u>. (2 syllables)

  When 'ed' is added to the word visi<u>t</u> (2 syllables), visit<u>ed</u> is pronounced visit<u>ed</u>. (3 syllables)

Irregular past tense verbs

In some English words, instead of adding 'ed', a change is made to the spelling of the word. These verbs are called *irregular* past tense.

Write the irregular past tense of the following words. They are all in Conversation 1 (page 68).

bend	_____	think	_____	are	_____
keep	_____	bite	_____	is	_____
spit	_____	go	_____	catch	_____

You can check the answers on page 120.

See list of irregular past tense verbs on page 75.

B) Discourse markers in storytelling

Discourse markers are expressions used to show connection between what has been said (or written) and what we will say (or write) next. Find the discourse markers below (1, 2, 3, 4,) in Conversation 1, page 68.

1. **'You'll never guess what happened,'** is used to get attention and to introduce a recount story.

2. **'Well, as you know,...'** is used to review information that the speakers already know because it is relevant to the story they are now going to tell.

3. **'Anyway, ...'** is used to introduce what happened next when telling a story.

4. **'And...?'** is used to show interest and ask what happened next in a story (often spoken with rising intonation).

See more about discourse markers on page 89.

FOCUS ON SPOKEN LANGUAGE

C) 'So' and 'Such' used to add emphasis

- 'So' can be used <u>before adjectives</u> (without nouns) to mean 'very'; to add emphasis or attention to the meaning of the adjective.

  eg. 'She's <u>so</u> happy.' 'He's <u>so</u> quiet.' 'You're <u>so</u> jealous!'

- 'Such' can be used before a noun phrase (a + adjective + noun), to add emphasis to the meaning of the adjective.

  eg. 'This is <u>such</u> a beautiful place.' 'He's <u>such</u> a clever child.' It's <u>such</u> a cold day!

  Note: It is <u>not</u> possible to use 'such' in this way with '<u>the</u> + adjective + noun'.

Practice

Complete the sentences from Conversation 1 (page 68), by adding 'so' or 'such' in the appropriate places.

Kim:... It's been _____ busy.

Kim: But I thought he was _____ a show-off; and always _____ full of himself!

Kim: He said he was very taken with my work and that I'd been _____ a good sport through a very busy time.

You can check your answers on page 120.

Reference page - A list of some irregular past tense verbs

base verb infinitive present simple	past simple	past participle * for the present perfect tense, use with *have/has* * for the past perfect use *had*
be/am/is/are	was/were	been
beat	beat	beaten
become	became	become
begin	began	begun
bend	bent	bent
bite	bit	bitten
blow	blew	blown
break	broke	broken
bring	brought	brought
build	built	built
burn	burned/burnt	burned/burnt
buy	bought	bought
catch	caught	caught
choose	chose	chosen
come	came	come
dig	dug	dug
do	did	done
draw	drew	drawn
drink	drank	drunk
drive	drove	driven
eat	ate	eaten
fall	fell	fallen
feed	fed	fed
feel	felt	felt
fight	fought	fought
find	found	found
fly	flew	flown
forget	forgot	forgotten
forgive	forgave	forgiven
get	got	got (US = gotten)
give	gave	given
go	went	gone
grow	grew	grown
have	had	had
hear	heard	heard
hide	hid	hidden
hold	held	held
keep	kept	kept
know	knew	known
lay	laid	laid
lead	led	led
leave	left	left

base verb infinitive present simple	past simple	past participle * for the present perfect tense, use with *have/has* * for the past perfect use *had*
lend	lent	lent
light	lit	lit
lose	lost	lost
make	made	made
mean	meant	meant
meet	met	met
pay	paid	paid
read /ri:d/*	read /red/	read /red/
ride	rode	ridden
ring	rang	rung
rise	rose	risen
run	ran	run
say	said	said
see	saw	seen
sell	sold	sold
send	sent	sent
show	showed	shown
sing	sang	sung
sink	sank	sunk
sit	sat	sat
sleep	slept	slept
speak	spoke	spoken
spell	spelt/spelled	spelt/spelled
spend	spent	spent
spring	sprang	sprung
stand	stood	stood
steal	stole	stolen
sting	stung	stung
swear	swore	sworn
swim	swam	swum
swing	swung	swung
take	took	taken
teach	taught	taught
tear /teə(r)/	tore	torn
tell	told	told
think	thought	thought
throw	threw	thrown
understand	understood	understood
wake	woke	woken
wear	wore	worn
win	won	won
write	wrote	written

* For an explanation of pronunciation symbols, refer to phonemic chart at the back of this book.

(Units 4 - 6)

This section reviews some of the expressions that were introduced in Units 4, 5, and 6 and gives you a chance to see what you have remembered.

Look at the pictures on the opposite page and decide what the people are saying by choosing from the expressions below.

Match each picture with an appropriate expression by writing the correct letter in the box next to each expression.

For extra practice, you could write the appropriate expression in the space provided in the picture.

1) I've got a lot on my plate and I'm on edge. ☐

2) He's pulling your leg. He's my cousin, not my brother. ☐

3) You won't be all smiles if you spill that milk. You'll change your tune then! ☐

4) I haven't made up my mind what I'll have to eat yet. ☐

5) They were taken with each other from the word go. ☐

6) Look at her. She's so full of herself! ☐

7) My neighbour keeps tabs on me every time I leave the house. ☐

8) I shouldn't have done that. I have a thing about heights. ☐

9) The insurance money will be a drop in the ocean. ☐

(Answers: page 120)

(Units 4 - 6)

UNIT 7

TALKING ABOUT SOCIAL ISSUES

The term 'social Issues' refers to problems or situations within a society that may affect a large number of people.

In this unit you will listen to a conversation between friends who are talking about social issues.

Pre Listening - Part 1

Before listening, check the following words in a dictionary. Match each word to its meaning. One has been done as an example. Answers, page 120.

judge	~~attitude~~	depressing
advantage	ignore	

1. the opinions and feelings that you have about something   _attitude_

2. decide or give an opinion about whether something is right or wrong   _____

3. making you feel sad   _____

4. to <u>not</u> give attention to something   _____

5. something that helps you do things well and be successful   _____

Listening for general understanding

The conversation contains colloquial expressions that will be explained later in the unit, so don't worry if you don't understand every word. This time you are listening for general understanding of the topic. As you listen, tick the correct answers below. Then check your answers on page 120.

1) Why is Dan doing social work?

          a) because he likes helping people

          b) because he earns a lot of money doing it

2) Karen thinks:

          a) everyone should be responsible for themselves

          b) the government should help people with problems

3) Dan thinks:

          a) everyone should do social work on the weekend

          b) people who have advantages should help those who don't (have advantages)

4) At the end of the conversation Dan and Karen:

          a) agree that people should be helped to help themselves

          b) agree that people should work harder

> Now we'll look at the everyday expressions used in the conversation – turn to the next page.

CONVERSATION 1 (with everyday expressions)

◄◄ Replay Conversation 1
Read this conversation as you listen to the audio recording. Do you know what the _underlined_ words mean? They are colloquial or everyday expressions.

Karen: Dan I think it's great that you're doing social work but ….

Dan: But what?

Karen: Well, isn't it depressing spending all day with people who are **down and out**?

Dan: Sometimes…but I like helping people. Besides, just because something's depressing, doesn't mean we can **sweep it under the carpet**.

Karen: Yes but don't you think people with problems **bring it on themselves** through their own bad decisions and then expect other people to **pick up the pieces**.

Dan: Sometimes… not always. Take me, when I got sick last year. When I was **at a low ebb**, I needed a bit of help to get through it and **get back on my feet**.

Karen: Yes but that's different, you were sick. But _generally_, I think everyone should be responsible for themselves. You know the saying: **'The buck stops here'**. We have to help ourselves.

Dan: Mm. Yes but it's not that simple. Life isn't **black and white**. We can't judge someone when we don't know all the **ins and outs** of the situation.

Karen: What do you mean?

Dan: Well, sometimes people **get a raw deal**. They get sick, they lose their job; **one thing leads to another** and they get into debt, they get depressed and then they **can't get out of the rut** and get another job. It's **a vicious circle**.

Karen: Yes but everyone has **ups and downs**. **That's life**. I lost my job once but I didn't go round with **a chip on my shoulder**. I just had to **get on with it** and get another job.

Dan: Yes but how did you get another job?

Karen: Oh a friend **pulled strings** for me to get a job in her company.

Dan: And that's my point - your friend **looked out for** you. And that's how it should be in society – people who have advantages should help those who don't. If we just **turn our back on** social problems, they'll just get worse. It's **a chain reaction**.

Karen: OK, **I see what you're getting at** and I agree; social problems won't go away by **turning a blind eye**. But my point is, wouldn't it be better to help people to help themselves?

Dan: I couldn't agree more. That way's better for everyone……

Now let's see what these expressions mean - look at the next page.

CONVERSATION 2 (explanation of everyday expressions)

Compare Conversation 1 with Conversation 2 -You will see that some of the words are different but the meaning is the same in both conversations. Find the underlined words in Conversation 1, then underline the words with the same meaning in Conversation 2.
For example: <u>down and out</u> (Conversation 1) = <u>very poor, with no job</u> (Conversation 2)

Karen: Dan I think it's great that you're doing social work but ….

Dan: But what?

Karen: Well, isn't it depressing spending all day with people who are <u>very poor, with no job</u>?

Dan: Sometimes… but I like helping people. Besides, just because something's depressing, doesn't mean we can try to hide or forget about the problem.

Karen: Yes but don't you think people with problems cause the problem for themselves through their own bad decisions and then expect other people to fix the problem after a difficult situation.

Dan: Sometimes… not always. Take me, when I got sick last year. When I was feeling depressed, unhappy, I needed a bit of help to get through it and become independent again.

Karen: Yes but that's different, you were sick. But *generally*, I think everyone should be responsible for themselves. You know the saying: 'I'm responsible for the result of my decision'. We have to help ourselves.

Dan: Mm. Yes but it's not that simple. Life isn't simple with issues being completely right or completely wrong. We can't judge someone when we don't know all the details of the situation.

Karen: What do you mean?

Dan: Well, sometimes people are treated unfairly. They get sick, they lose their job; one situation causes another situation and they get into debt, they get depressed and then they can't change the bad situation and get another job. It's a situation in which one problem creates more problems.

Karen: Yes but everyone has good and bad experiences. We must accept the things that happen. I lost my job once but I didn't go round with an angry attitude. I just had to continue my usual activities and get another job.

Dan: Yes but how did you get another job?

Karen: Oh a friend used her influence with important people for me to get a job in her company.

Dan: And that's my point - your friend helped and cared for you. And that's how it should be in society – people who have advantages should help those who don't. If we just ignore social problems, they'll just get worse. It's a situation where one situation causes another situation.

Karen: OK, I understand what you're explaining and I agree; social problems won't go away by ignoring (something) because you don't want to do anything about it. But my point is, wouldn't it be better to help people to help themselves?

Dan: I couldn't agree more. That way's better for everyone……

Now to become familiar with the everyday expressions, practise CONVERSATION 1 aloud with a partner.

◄◄ **Replay Conversation 1**
Listen to the conversation again and fill in the missing words. You may need to listen more than once. (Don't worry about your spelling as this activity focuses on listening skills; you can check your spelling later.)

Karen: Dan I think it's great that you're doing social work but ….

Dan: But what?

Karen: Well, isn't it depressing spending all day with people who are <u>down and</u> _____?

Dan: Sometimes…but I like helping people. Besides, just because something's depressing, doesn't mean we can <u>sweep it</u> _____ <u>the carpet</u>.

Karen: Yes but don't you think people with problems <u>bring it</u> _____ <u>themselves</u> through their own bad decisions and then expect other people to _____ <u>up the pieces</u>.

Dan: Sometimes… not always. Take me, when I got sick last year. When I was <u>at a</u> _____ <u>ebb</u>, I needed a bit of help to get through it and <u>get back on my</u> _____.

Karen: Yes but that's different, you were sick. But *generally*, I think everyone should be responsible for themselves. You know the saying: '<u>The buck stops</u> _____'. We have to help ourselves.

Dan: Mm. Yes but it's not that simple. Life isn't _____ <u>and white</u>. We can't judge someone when we don't know all the _____ <u>and outs</u> of the situation.

Karen: What do you mean?

Dan: Well, sometimes people <u>get a</u> _____ <u>deal</u>. They get sick, they lose their job; <u>one thing</u> _____ <u>to another</u> and they get into debt, they get depressed and then they <u>can't get</u> _____ <u>of the rut</u> and get another job. It's <u>a vicious</u> _____.

Karen: Yes but everyone has _____ <u>and downs</u>. <u>That's life</u>. I lost my job once but I didn't go round with <u>a</u> _____ <u>on my shoulder</u>. I just had to <u>get on with it</u> and get another job.

Dan: Yes but how did you get another job?

Karen: Oh a friend _____ <u>strings</u> for me to get a job in her company.

Dan: And that's my point - your friend <u>looked out</u> _____ you. And that's how it should be in society – people who have advantages should help those who don't. If we just <u>turn our back</u> _____ social problems, they'll just get worse. It's <u>a</u> _____ <u>reaction</u>.

Karen: OK, <u>I see what you're</u> _____ <u>at</u> and I agree; social problems won't go away by <u>turning a blind</u> _____. But my point is, wouldn't it be better to help people to help themselves?

Dan: I couldn't agree more. That way's better for everyone……

Now check your answers by comparing this page with
CONVERSATION 1.

In order to become more familiar with these new everyday expressions:

◀◀ Replay Conversation 1

    1) Listen and tick the boxes ✓ next to the expressions as you hear them.
    2) Write the definitions you can remember. One has been done for you as example.
    3) Check your answers by turning to page 130.

☐	down and out	*very poor, with no job*
☐	sweep it under the carpet*............	_____
☐	bring it on themselves...............	_____
☐	pick up the pieces....................	_____
☐	at a low ebb............................	_____
☐	get back on my feet..................	_____
☐	'The buck stops here'...................	_____
☐	black and white..........................	_____
☐	ins and outs	_____
☐	get a raw deal..........................	_____
☐	one thing leads to another...........	_____
☐	can't get out of the rut.................	_____
☐	a vicious circle.........................	_____
☐	ups and downs.........................	_____
☐	That's life!..............................	_____
☐	a chip on my shoulder.................	_____
☐	get on with it...........................	_____
☐	pulled strings*..........................	_____
☐	looked out for*..........................	_____
☐	turn our back on........................	_____
☐	a chain reaction........................	_____
☐	I see what you're getting at..........	_____
☐	turning a blind eye.....................	_____

LANGUAGE NOTES

* The expression 'sweep it under the carpet' can also be expressed as 'sweep it under the rug'.

* The expression 'pull strings' means use your influence to get something. However, 'pull <u>the</u> strings' of something or someone means to control what an organisation or person does. eg. Tom is very young but <u>he pulls the strings of</u> a very large company.

* When we say we 'look out for' someone, it means to help and care for someone. However, the expression 'look out for <u>number one</u>' means to do only what is best for yourself and not care about other people.

CROSSWORD - LANGUAGE REVIEW

Complete the sentences, choosing from the everyday expressions that are listed below. You can use the clues in brackets ( ) at the end of each sentence to help you. Then complete the crossword using the everyday expressions you have written. One has been done as an example.

chip on his shoulder	~~turn a blind eye~~	turn our backs	black and white
pick up the pieces	down and out	ups and downs	
look out for	sweep it under the carpet	low ebb	pull strings

ACROSS

1) We can't continue to **_turn a blind eye_** to the problems in our hospitals. (ignore)

3) Discipline in school is not a _____ _____ _____ issue. (a simple issue of right or wrong)

5) I remember when I was _____ _____ _____. I couldn't pay my rent. (very poor, no job)

7) Poverty is a big problem. We can't _____ _____ _____ _____ _____. (try to hide it)

9) Can you _____ _____ and get some free tickets to the concert? (use your influence)

11) He has a _____ _____ _____ _____ because he's divorced. (an angry & resentful attitude)

DOWN

2) I'm the oldest in the family so I always _____ _____ _____ my younger sisters. (help, care for)

4) Everyone has _____ _____ _____ throughout their life. (good and bad experiences)

6) After the fire we had to _____ ___ _____ _____ and rebuild our home. (fix the problem)

8) We're upset by our son's problem but we can't _____ _____ _____ on him. (ignore)

10) When I was at a _____ _____ , friends were there to help me. (feeling depressed, unhappy)

Answers, page 120.

FOCUS ON SPOKEN LANGUAGE

A) Giving conversational feedback

When having a conversation in English, it is very important to give 'feedback'. This involves using expressions that show we are listening and understand what our partner is saying. We do this by using expressions such as: 'Yes', 'Yes but...', 'Mm....', 'OK', 'Well....', 'I see what you mean.....', 'I see what you're getting at', etc.

Check Conversation 1 (page 80) to see where the speakers gave conversational feedback by using some of the expressions above.

This is an important aspect of spoken English as a conversation could sound abrupt or unnatural without such expressions. In some cultures this aspect of communication is not so important, but when communicating in English, it is necessary to give feedback to show you are interested and understand what has been said.

Disagreeing Politely

When disagreeing with another person's opinion, we can begin by saying 'Yes, but...' to **show that we have listened** to the other person's opinion before giving a different opinion.

Read Conversation 1 (page 80) again and note three sentences where the speakers use 'Yes, but...' to disagree politely before introducing a different opinion.

1. _____

2. _____

3. _____

(Answers: page 121)

Non-verbal Feedback

We also use non-verbal feedback such as smiling and nodding our head (up and down) when we agree with what is being said, or by frowning and shaking our head (side to side) if we hear bad news, don't understand or disagree with the speaker.

When a person has no expression on their face or gives no feedback to show that they are listening and interested, this expression is called 'deadpan', meaning they don't show any feeling or expression on their face. This lack of expression can give the message that they are not interested. So remember it's important to give feedback - with our words and our face!

For examples of agreeing and disagreeing politely see 'Conversation Strategies - Agreeing and Disagreeing Politely' on page 88.

FOCUS ON SPOKEN LANGUAGE

B) As the saying goes:

As discussed in Unit 3 (page 37), a 'saying' is a short, well-known statement that expresses a meaning or idea that most people believe is true and wise.
For example in Conversation 1 Karen says: 'The buck stops here.'

Here are some more 'sayings'. What do you think they mean? Choose the correct 'meaning' below and write it next to the appropriate 'saying'. You can check your answers on page 121.

Saying	**Meaning**
1) 'There's no such thing as a free lunch.'	_____
2) 'You can't judge a book by its cover.'	_____
3) 'Every cloud has a silver lining.'	_____

Meanings

a) Every bad situation has some benefit or good side-effect.

b) Don't judge someone or something by appearance only because you may be wrong.

c) You can not expect to be given things for nothing as things need to be paid for or worked for.

C) Grammar - Reflexive pronouns

We use reflexive pronouns such as (herself, himself, themselves,) when the subject and object of a sentence are the same person or persons.
Look at these examples

subject   object

Susan is looking at **herself**.

John is looking at **himself**.

They are looking at **themselves**.

Subject pronoun	Reflexive pronoun	Subject pronoun	Reflexive pronoun
I	**myself**	we	**ourselves**
you (singular)	**yourself**	you (plural)	**yourselves**
she	**herself**	they	**themselves**
he	**himself**	it	**itself**

1) Complete these sentences with a reflexive pronoun. Check your answers on page 121.

a) The little boy is too small to feed _____. His mother has to feed him.

b) You'll have to cook dinner for _____ tonight. I'm not going to be here.

Note: The expressions 'by myself', 'by yourself' means 'alone'. eg. I live by myself. = I live alone.

FOCUS ON SPOKEN LANGUAGE

Reflexive pronouns (continued)

We also use reflexive pronouns to emphasise that we think a person or people should do something and not let other people do it for them. Examples of this are used in Conversation 1.

2) Find these sentences on page 80 and complete the sentences with the appropriate pronoun.

a) I think everyone should be responsible for _____.

b) We have to help _____.

c) ...my point is, wouldn't it be better to help people to help _____?

Answers, page 121.

D) Asking an opinion with a negative question

Asking an opinion with a negative question suggests that the answer will be 'yes' and therefore invites agreement. For example, we say, 'Isn't it a lovely day?' expecting the answer to be 'Yes'.

Karen uses this conversation strategy when talking to Dan about social issues. She wants him to agree with her opinion. Check Conversation 1 (page 80) and complete the questions.

1) Well, _____ spending all day with people who are down and out?

2) Yes but _____ people with problems bring it on themselves?

3) But my point is, _____ to help people to help themselves?

Answers, page 121.

You will notice in Conversation 1 that although Karen wanted Dan to agree with her opinion, he did <u>not</u> agree with Karen's opinion every time.

It's important to know how to disagree politely when having a conversation. Look at page 88 for examples of ways to agree, disagree, check meaning and be neutral (neutral means not agreeing with either side of an issue or argument.)

E) Incomplete sentences in spoken language

In conversational speech, speakers do not always use complete sentences. In fact, words are often left out if the meaning is clear without using a complete sentence. This aspect of language is referred to in grammar books as '*ellipsis*'.
When writing, three dots (...) are often used to show that words have been left out of a sentence.

Sometimes speakers don't finish a sentence because they are hesitant; not sure how it will be interpreted. They don't want to offend their partner.

Read Karen's first sentence from Conversation 1.

Dan I think it's great that you're doing social work but...

Why do you think Karen didn't complete her sentence? Check your answer on page 121.

Conversation strategies

Agreeing and disagreeing politely, asking for clarification and staying neutral

When discussing issues with family, friends or work associates, we don't always agree with each other. Therefore, it's important to express an opinion in a way that doesn't lead to an argument.

The following reference lists show expressions used when agreeing, staying neutral, disagreeing or asking for clarification in a discussion.

Ways of agreeing	Ways of disagreeing
That's for sure! Absolutely! I couldn't agree more! (means: I agree 100%) Yes, I see what you mean. That's a good point. Yes, I agree. Yes, I'd have to agree with that.	Yes but… Yes, but I think … Yes, but on the other hand… Yes, but don't you think … You have a point but… I agree to an extent but… (means: I don't agree completely.) That may be the case, however… I see what you mean but… I see what you're getting at but…
Ways of expressing a neutral or uncertain position	**Ways of asking for clarification (checking meaning)**
Maybe, but… Maybe, maybe not. Perhaps… Who knows? (means 'I don't know the answer') Yes and no. (when there isn't a clear answer to a question) I can see it from both sides.	Sorry, I'm not sure what you mean. Sorry, I didn't catch that. Do you mean that… Sorry, I'm not sure what you are getting at. Pardon?

When disagreeing with another person's opinion, beginning with '*Yes, but…*' demonstrates politeness by **showing that you have listened** to the other person's opinion before giving a different opinion.

Discourse markers are expressions used to show connection between what has already been said (or written) and what we will say (or write) next.

In spoken English, discourse markers also indicate the attitude of the speaker to what is being said and prepare the listener for what will be said next. Some expressions are more common in informal conversation and others are more likely to be used in formal situations such as lectures or reports. Some examples are given below.

More informal
general conversation

More formal
speeches, lectures, reports

Introducing a story or opinion

More informal	More formal
You'll never guess what's happened!	I'm going to talk about...
In my opinion,...	Consider the fact that,...
If you ask me,...	Firstly, it appears...

Focussing attention

More informal	More formal
The main thing is....	An important point is...
Let's face it!	It is important to realise...
As a matter of fact,	In fact,...
You know...	With regard to...
Speaking of...	With reference to...

Clarifying information

More informal	More formal
What I mean is...	In other words,
What I'm getting at is...	That is to say...

Generalising

More informal	More formal
As a rule...	In most cases...
On the whole...	In general,...
...and so on	...etcetera

Changing the subject

More informal	More formal
By the way,	On a different subject...
While I think of it...	

Adding information

More informal	More formal
On top of that	In addition...
and what's more...	Furthermore...
Besides that...	Additionally,

Summarising or concluding

More informal	More formal
To cut a long story short...	In summary,
And in the end...	In conclusion,
When all is said and done...	All things considered...
Having said all that,...	

As noted in the introduction, our choice of words is always dependent on the context or situation in which it is used. Therefore, when learning a new language, it is necessary to become familiar with the different contexts in which certain expressions are used before beginning to use them.

UNIT 8

THE MEDIA

The media is defined as: 'all the organisations, such as television, radio and newspapers that provide news and information for the public.'

Longman Dictionary of Contemporary English (2003)

In this unit you will listen to a conversation between friends who are talking about the media (Unit 8 on the audio recording). The conversation contains everyday expressions that will be explained later in the unit - so don't worry if you don't understand every word. This time you are listening for general understanding of the topic.

Part 1 - Pre Listening

Before listening, match the following words with the definitions below. Answers, page 121.

a journalist	be objective	fact	fiction	be responsible
least	powerful	disadvantages	celebrities	exposing

1. someone who writes information or stories for newspapers or TV _____

2. information that is true _____   3. not a true story _____

4. having power over people _____   5. showing or uncovering_____

6. think/act only on fact, not feelings _____   7. famous people _____

8. be wise, careful and correct _____   9. less than anything else_____

10. negative points _____

Listening for general understanding

Now listen to the conversation and choose the correct answers below. Answers, page 121.

1) What does Paul say he likes best about his job as a journalist:

        a) travelling to different places.

        b) exciting stories, getting the answers to problems and exposing a cover-up.

2) What does Paul say he likes least about his job?

        a) getting information about celebrities just to sell a story

        b) when a situation is difficult to report objectively.

        c) travelling to different places.

3) Regarding the media, Kylie says:

        a) We shouldn't believe everything we read or see on TV.

        b) The media spends a lot of money.

Now we'll look at the everyday expressions used in the conversation – turn to the next page.

CONVERSATION 1 (with everyday expressions)

◄◄ Replay Conversation 1
Read this conversation as you listen to the audio recording. Do you know what the _underlined_ words mean? They are colloquial or everyday expressions.

Kylie: I hear you're a journalist now Paul. That must be exciting.

Paul: Yeah. It's **a buzz** most of the time but like all jobs, it has its **drawbacks**.

Kylie: I guess so. So what do you like best about your job?

Paul: Oh, I like being **in the thick of** an exciting story; **getting to the bottom of** a problem; you know, exposing **a cover-up**.

Kylie: Mm I can understand that. And what do you like least?

Paul: I'd say **digging up dirt** on celebrities just to sell a story. .. or when a situation is **close to home** - it can be difficult to report it objectively.

Kylie: You mean if a story **touches a nerve**.

Paul: Well yes, you get used to it, but if you feel really strongly about something it's difficult to be objective about it.

Kylie: Yes I suppose it'd be difficult to be objective about every story.

Paul: It is. And when you think about it, the media reaches so many people and can be very powerful; responsible reporting is so important. And there can be **a fine line between** fact and fiction.

Kylie: Mm, and I guess it can be a problem if people believe everything they see on TV or read in the newspaper.

Paul: That's right. Sometimes people don't see there may be **a hidden agenda** in a news report.

Kylie: Especially if it's **to do with** politics or **big business**.

Paul: That's right. On the other hand, the media can act as **a watchdog**, making sure politicians and big business **toe the line**. Some organisations or governments would **get away with murder** if the media wasn't **keeping an eye on** them.

Kylie: Yes but as you just said, the media has a lot of power. When telling a story, reporters can **put it in a good light** or **put it in a bad light**.

Paul: And that's why people have to **read between the lines** and try to get more than one side to a story. Don't forget, the media needs interesting stories to sell newspapers. And some journalists will **stop at nothing** to make a story interesting even if it means **bending the truth**.

Kylie: Mm. I see your point.

Paul: **Having said all that**, **on the whole** I think the media is a very necessary part of today's world, don't you?

Kylie: Absolutely. We need to know what's happening in the world but we also need to read between the lines and be careful not to believe everything we read or see on TV.

Paul: **I couldn't have put it better myself**. Anyway, that's enough about me. Tell me about...

Now let's see what these expressions mean - look at the next page.

CONVERSATION 2 (explanation of everyday expressions)

Compare Conversation 1 with Conversation 2 -You will see that some of the words are different but the meaning is the same in both conversations. Find the underlined words in Conversation 1, then underline the words with the same meaning in Conversation 2.
For example: a buzz (Conversation 1) = an exciting feeling (Conversation 2)

Kylie: I hear you're a journalist now Paul. That must be exciting.

Paul: Yeah. It's <u>an exciting feeling</u> most of the time but like all jobs, it has its disadvantages.

Kylie: I guess so. So what do you like best about your job?

Paul: Oh, I like being very involved in an exciting story; finding the answer to a problem; you know, exposing something that has been kept as a secret from people.

Kylie: Mm. I can understand that. And what do you like least?

Paul: I'd say finding bad information on celebrities just to sell a story... or when a situation makes me uncomfortable because it affects me personally - it can be difficult to report it objectively.

Kylie: You mean if a story is upsetting for you.

Paul: Well yes, you get used to it, but if you feel really strongly about something it's difficult to be objective about it.

Kylie: Yes I suppose it'd be difficult to be objective about every story.

Paul: It is. And when you think about it, the media reaches so many people and can be very powerful; responsible reporting is so important. And there can be only a very small difference between fact and fiction.

Kylie: Mm, and I guess it can be a problem if people believe everything they see on TV or read in the newspaper.

Paul: That's right. Sometimes people don't see there may be a different meaning to the one openly spoken about in a news report.

Kylie: Especially if it's relating to politics or large, powerful companies.

Paul: That's right. On the other hand, the media can act as a group that make sure companies act legally, making sure politicians and big business behave in the correct way. Some organisations or governments would do whatever they wanted to without control or punishment if the media wasn't carefully watching them.

Kylie: Yes but as you just said, the media has a lot of power. When telling a story, reporters can present the situation as a good thing or present it as a bad thing.

Paul: And that's why people have to try to understand the *real* meaning and not just what is written or said and try to get more than one side to a story. Don't forget, the media needs interesting stories to sell newspapers. And some journalists will do anything to make a story interesting even if it means saying something that is not completely true.

Kylie: Mm. I see your point.

Paul: However in summary, generally I think the media is a very necessary part of today's world, don't you?

Kylie: Absolutely. We need to know what's happening in the world but we also need to read between the lines and be careful not to believe everything we read or see on TV.

Paul: I agree completely. Anyway, that's enough about me. Tell me about...

> Now to become familiar with the everyday expressions,
> practise reading CONVERSATION 1 aloud with a partner.

◄◄ Replay Conversation 1

Listen to the conversation again and fill in the missing words. You may need to listen more than once. (Don't worry about your spelling as this activity focuses on listening skills; you can check your spelling later.)

Kylie: I hear you're a journalist now Paul. That must be exciting.

Paul: Yeah. It's <u>a buzz</u> most of the time but like all jobs, it has its <u>drawbacks</u>.

Kylie: I guess so. So what do you like best about your job?

Paul: Oh, I like being <u>in the _____</u> of an exciting story; <u>getting to the _____</u> of a problem; you know, exposing <u>a cover-____</u>.

Kylie: Mm I can understand that. And what do you like least?

Paul: I'd say <u>digging up _____</u> on celebrities just to sell a story. .. or when a situation is <u>close to _____</u>- it can be difficult to report it objectively.

Kylie: You mean if a story <u>touches a _____</u>?

Paul: Well yes, you get used to it, but if you feel really strongly about something it's difficult to be objective about it.

Kylie: Yes I suppose it'd be difficult to be objective about every story.

Paul: It is. And when you think about it, the media reaches so many people and can be very powerful; responsible reporting is so important. And there can be <u>a fine _____</u> <u>between</u> fact and fiction.

Kylie: Mm, and I guess it can be a problem if people believe everything they see on TV or read in the newspaper.

Paul: That's right. Sometimes people don't see there may be <u>a _____</u> agenda in a news report.

Kylie: Especially if it's <u>to do_____</u> politics or <u>_____</u> business.

Paul: That's right. On the other hand, the media can act as <u>a watch_____</u>, making sure politicians and big business <u>toe the _____</u>. Some organisations or governments would <u>get _____</u> with murder if the media wasn't <u>keeping an _____</u> on them.

Kylie: Yes but as you just said, the media has a lot of power. When telling a story, reporters can <u>_____ it in a good light</u> or <u>put it in a bad _____</u>.

Paul: And that's why people have to <u>read _____</u> the lines and try to get more than one side to a story. Don't forget, the media needs interesting stories to sell newspapers. And some journalists will <u>stop at _____</u> to make a story interesting even if it means <u>_____</u> the truth.

Kylie: Mm. I see your point.

Paul: <u>Having said _____ that</u>, <u>on the _____</u> I think the media is a very necessary part of today's world, don't you?

Kylie: Absolutely. We need to know what's happening in the world but we also need to read between the lines and be careful not to believe everything we read or see on TV.

Paul: <u>I couldn't have _____ it better myself</u>. Anyway, that's enough about me. Tell me about …

> Now check your answers by comparing this page with CONVERSATION 1.

In order to become more familiar with these new everyday expressions:

◄◄ Replay Conversation 1

1) Listen and tick the boxes ☑ next to the expressions as you hear them.
2) Write the definitions you can remember. One has been done for you as an example.
3) Check your answers by turning to page 131.

☐ a buzz* .... *an exciting feeling* _____

☐ drawbacks .... _____

☐ in the thick of........................... _____

☐ getting to the bottom of............... _____

☐ a cover-up. .... _____

☐ digging up dirt …..................... _____

☐ close to home......................... _____

☐ touches a nerve*....................... _____

☐ a fine line between.................... _____

☐ a hidden agenda .... _____

☐ to do with .... _____

☐ big business ....….. _____

☐ a watchdog............................ _____

☐ toe the line ....…............. _____

☐ get away with murder .... _____

☐ keeping an eye on .... _____

☐ put it in a good light .... _____

☐ put it in a bad light................. _____

☐ read between the lines............... _____

☐ stop at nothing.......…....…........ _____

☐ bending the truth .... _____

☐ Having said all that .... _____

☐ on the whole ....….. _____

☐ I couldn't have put it better myself. _____

LANGUAGE NOTE

* The expression 'a buzz' in Conversation 1 of this unit means 'an exciting feeling; a feeling of success'. However if you 'give someone a buzz', it can also mean you call them on the telephone. e.g. 'I'll give a buzz at lunch time tomorrow.'

* The expression 'touch a nerve' can be expressed as 'touch a raw nerve.

CROSSWORD - LANGUAGE REVIEW

Complete the sentences, choosing from the everyday expressions that are listed below. You can use the clues in brackets ( ) at the end of each sentence to help you. Then complete the crossword using the everyday expressions you have written. One has been done as an example.

~~get to the bottom~~	a hidden agenda	on the whole
bend the truth a fine line	get away with murder	read between the lines
stop at nothing	in a bad light	toe the line

ACROSS

1) It's important to **_get to the bottom_** of your money problem or it will get worse. (find the answer)

3) There's only___ _____ _____ between disagreement and argument. (a very small difference)

5) I never _____ _____ _____ about my tax bill. (say something that is not completely true)

7) Because he is famous, he thinks he can _____ _____ _____ _____. (do whatever he wants to without control or punishment)

9) It's important to _____ _____ _____ _____ of the company's report! (understand the *real* meaning)

DOWN

2) The newspaper put the story ___ ___ _____ _____. (presented it as a bad thing)

4) I think their plan has __ _____ _____. (a different meaning to the one spoken of)

6) He will _____ ___ _____ to get what he wants. (do anything)

8) There was a short storm but ____ _____ _____ the weather was fine. (generally)

10) If he doesn't _____ _____ _____, I'll ask him to leave.! (behave in the correct way)

Answers, page 122.

FOCUS ON SPOKEN LANGUAGE

A) The definite article 'the' - Review

Note: 'the' is discussed in more detail in Unit 4, page 49.

'The' is called the **definite article** because it can be used to talk about definite, specific, or unique things. For example, we use the definite article when a thing or group of things is considered to be **unique.** Some examples used in Conversation 1 are: **the** truth, **the** media.

There are also some specific expressions with 'the'.
Check Conversation 1 (page 92) and complete the
expressions below.

1) I like being in _____ _____ of an exciting story; getting to _____ _____ of a problem.

2) On_____ _____ _____, the media can act as a watchdog, making sure politicians and

   big business toe _____ _____.

3) …people have to read between _____ _____ and try to get more than one side to a story.

4) …some journalists will stop at nothing to make a story interesting even if it means bending

   _____ _____.

Answers, page 122.

B) That

'**That**' can be used to make a connection with an earlier statement.

For example: 'I read a story about Spain. That's why I want to go there'.

'I missed the train. That's why I'm late.'

'**That**' can also be used at the beginning of a sentence to refer to something which is understood by the speakers to mean *'the situation we are talking about'*

For example: 'They had an accident.'   'Oh, <u>that</u>'s terrible!' ('That' refers to the accident.)

Examples

Look at the following examples from Conversation 1. What does *'that'* refer to in the sentences?

1. Kylie: ' I hear you're a journalist now Paul. <u>That</u> must be exciting.' (line 1)

   That refers to _____

2. Paul: And <u>that</u>'s why people have to read between the lines. (line 25)

   That refers to _____

Answers, page 122

C) Open ended questions

In Conversation 1, Kylie asked Paul 'open-ended' questions about his job. Open ended questions invite a person to give an answer with some details, rather than a short 'yes' or 'no' reply.

There are some examples of open-ended questions at the beginning of Conversation 1.

FOCUS ON SPOKEN LANGUAGE

C) Open ended questions (continued)

What questions does Kylie ask Paul at the beginning of Conversation 1? Answers, page 122

1. _____

2. _____

What other questions could you ask about someone's job to keep the conversation going?

D) You get used to it.

The expression 'used to' in the sentence, 'You get <u>used to</u> it.' means 'You become experienced in this situation so that it is no longer surprising, difficult or strange.'

In Conversation 1 (page 92) Paul uses the expression, 'you get used to it', to say that he is experienced in reporting situations and stories that 'touch a nerve' or are upsetting. Check conversation 1 and complete the following sentence:

Paul: Well yes, _____ but if you feel really strongly about something
it's difficult to be objective about it.

Note: In the sentence above, Paul uses the pronoun 'you' to generalise about the situation; to mean 'anyone in this situation'. The pronoun 'one' is a more formal way of expressing 'anyone in this situation'. Compare the following two sentences as an example:

'*One* gets used to flying if *one* does it often'. (more formal, not generally used in conversational speech)

'*You* get used to flying if *you* do it often'. (used more generally in conversational speech)

Note: The expression **'used to + <u>verb</u>'** has a different function to that explained above and refers
to an activity that happened regularly in the past but does not happen now.
verb
eg. I <u>used to</u> <u>do</u> a lot of painting but I'm too busy now.

See 'Understanding Everyday Australian - Book Two', 'Unit 7 - Talking about the Past' to learn more about this structure.

E) Uses of the verb 'get'

'Get' is one of the most widely used verbs in spoken English and is used in a variety of ways.

Find two sentences with 'get' in Conversation 1 (page 92). Complete the sentences below.

1. Paul: Oh, I like being in the thick of an exciting story; _____

2. Paul: Some organisations or governments would _____
if the media wasn't keeping an eye on them.

See page 99 for a list of 'phrasal verbs' with 'get'.
For general information about 'phrasal verbs' see page 54.

Reference Page – Examples of phrasal verbs with 'get'

get across (an idea) means succeed in making people understand, eg. I must get across my idea.

get ahead means to progress financially or in your career, eg. He'll get ahead if he works hard.

get along means progressing with a situation in your life, eg. How 're you getting along with the diet?

get along with (someone) means have a friendly relationship, eg. I get along with John now.

get on with (someone) means the same as 'get along' (above) eg. I get on with all my neighbours.

get on with (an activity) means continue doing it, eg. 'I can't talk now, I have to get on with my work'.

get around (a difficulty) means to find a way to avoid it, eg. Don't worry. I'll get around the problem.

get around to (doing something) means doing it after a long delay. Did he get around to buying a car?

get at (something) means to reach it, eg. Keep your dictionary where you can easily get at it.

getting at (something) means explaining something, eg. Yes, I see what you're getting at now.

get away means to leave a place or go for a holiday, eg. 'I'm getting away for a week in July.'

get away with (something bad) means to do it but not be caught or punished, eg. He got away with it!

get back (somewhere) means to return there, eg. What time do you have to get back to the office?

get back at (someone) you punish them because they previously hurt you. 'I'll get back at him!'

get back into (an activity) means to start getting involved in it again. 'I'm getting back into sport.

get behind (with work) means you are slower or not making the same progress as other people.

get behind (someone/something) means support/ try to help it succeed, eg. Get behind your team!

get by means manage under difficult circumstances, eg. It's hard to get by without a job.

get down to (a job) means you start to do it attentively, eg. Let's get down to business.

get in on (an activity) means to start participating. 'Tell them you want to get in on the investment'.

get into (a subject) means to start getting interested in it, eg. I'm getting into tennis this year.

get off (a topic) means you change the topic of discussion, eg. I think we should get off this topic.

get off on (something) means to become excited by it, eg. He really gets off on rock-climbing.

get out of (doing something) means to avoid doing it, eg. 'He'll do anything to get out of helping.'

get over (a problem or illness) means to recover from it, eg. He'll never get over the accident.

get through (an exam/difficult situation) means complete successfully, survive it, eg. We'll get through!

get together means to meet or spend time with friends, eg. Let's get together on Friday for lunch.

get up means get out of bed, eg. What time do you usually get up?

get with (**it**) you become aware of the latest events, ideas, fashion, eg. Get with it! Use solar power!

**This is not a complete list. For a complete list of phrasal verbs with 'get' check your dictionary
or a book specifically about 'phrasal verbs'.**

UNIT 9

BUSINESS NEGOTIATIONS

'Negotiations' are discussions between people or groups of people in order
to reach an agreement with them.

Pre-listening

In this unit you will listen to a conversation between people who are aiming to negotiate a deal. (Unit 9 on your audio recording). Before listening, check the following words in a dictionary. Match each word to its correct meaning. You can check your answers on page 123.

legal	investment	finances	a proposal	project
	a deal	risk	genuine	

1. buying something to make a profit later _____ 2. management of money_____

3. the possibility of a bad result _____ 4. relating to the law _____

5. work or activity done over a period of time_____ 6. a business agreement _____

7. a suggestion or offer (often written) _____ 8. honest or real, not fake _____

Part 1 - Listening for general understanding

The conversation contains colloquial expressions that will be explained later in the unit, so don't worry if you don't understand every word. This time you are listening for general understanding of the topic. As you listen, tick the correct answers below. You can check your answers on page 123.

1) Ken calls Matt to ask about:

a) a building project

b) an investment project

2) Ken says he'd like to negotiate a lower price because:

a) there are some risks involved with the deal

b) he is having problems with his finances

3) With regard to the investment deal, Matt says:

a) There are several companies already interested.

b) He will consider selling at a lower price.

> Now we'll look at the everyday expressions used in the conversation – turn to the next page.

CONVERSATION 1 (with everyday expressions)

◀◀ Replay Conversation 1
Read this conversation as you listen to the audio recording. Do you know what the _underlined_ words mean? They are colloquial or everyday expressions.

Matt: Hello. Matt Thomas speaking.

Ken: Hello Matt, it's Ken Brown here.

Matt: G'day, Ken. How're you going?

Ken: Not bad, thanks. Look I hear you have an investment project **in the pipeline**.

Matt: That's right, yes. You're **quick off the mark**. We've only just re-advertised it.

Ken: Well we're always **on the lookout for** good investments and your proposal looks promising **on paper**. We haven't **gone over the fine print** yet though. But I have a few questions, if you don't mind.

Matt: Sure. Go ahead.

Ken: I heard there was a company interested in the investment but then the deal **fell through** before it was **wrapped up**?

Matt: That's right. The company was keen to **get in on the act** but there was **a question mark over** their finances.

Ken: I see.

Matt: They seemed **fair dinkum** at first but then we realised they were **playing for time** and so we **pulled the plug**.

Ken: **I get the picture**. So now you **are back to square one**?

Matt: Unfortunately yes. And we've wasted a bit of time already which has left us **out of pocket** so I'll **be up front** with you; we are keen to get moving on this.

Ken: Well as I said we're **in the market for** a good investment... So...

Matt: Well, **you've come to the right place** then.

Ken: Mm. **Just the same**, there'd be some risk involved from what I can see. We'd like to negotiate a lower price?

Matt: Not at this stage. Come on Ken; you know risk is always **part and parcel** of this kind of investment but believe me, deals like this one are **hard to come by**.

Ken: Mm.

Matt: And there are several other companies already interested, so if you **want a piece of the action** you'll have to **be first off the mark**.

Ken: OK. I'll talk to my partners and get back to you if we want to go any further. But thanks for your time Matt.

Matt: No worries Ken. Give my regards to Emma.

Ken: Will do. Bye Matt.

Now let's see what these expressions mean - look at the next page.

CONVERSATION 2 (explanation of everyday expressions)

*Compare Conversation 1 with Conversation 2 -*You will see that some of the words are different but the meaning is the same in both conversations. Find the underlined words in Conversation 1, then underline the words with the same meaning in Conversation 2.
For example: <u>in the pipeline</u> (Conversation 1) = (Conversation 2) <u>**that is being planned**</u>

Matt: Hello. Matt Thomas speaking.

Ken: Hello Matt, it's Ken Brown here.

Matt: G'day, Ken. How're you going?

Ken: Not bad, thanks. Look I hear you have an investment project <u>that is being planned</u>.

Matt: That's right, yes. You're quick to act on an opportunity. We've only just re-advertised it.

Ken: Well we're always searching for good investments and your proposal looks promising as a plan (but may not show the complete situation). We haven't checked the important legal information yet though. But I have a few questions if you don't mind.

Matt: Sure. Go ahead.

Ken: I heard there was a company interested in the investment but then the deal failed to happen before it was completed?

Matt: That's right. The company was keen to get involved in the activity but there was doubt about their finances.

Ken: I see.

Matt: They seemed genuine and honest at first but then we realised they were delaying doing something while they decided what to do and so we stopped the deal from continuing.

Ken: I understand the situation. So now you have to start again?

Matt: Unfortunately yes. And we've wasted a bit of time already which has left us with less money than we should have so I'll be clear and honest with you; we are keen to get moving on this.

Ken: Well as I said we're interested in buying a good investment... So…

Matt: Well, we have what you are looking for then.

Ken: Mm. However, there'd be some risk involved from what I can see. We'd like to negotiate a lower price?

Matt: Not at this stage. Come on Ken; you know risk is always an expected part of this kind of investment but believe me, deals like this one are difficult to find.

Ken: Mm.

Matt: And there are several other companies already interested, so if you want to get involved in this successful activity you'll have to act more quickly than anyone else.

Ken: OK I'll talk to my partners and get back to you if we want to go any further. But thanks for your time Matt.

Matt: No worries Ken. Give my regards to Emma.

Ken: Will do. Bye Matt.

> Now to become familiar with the everyday expressions,
> practise reading CONVERSATION 1 aloud with a partner.

◀◀ **Replay Conversation 1**
Listen to the conversation again and fill in the missing words. You may need to listen more than once. (Don't worry about your spelling as this activity focuses on listening skills; you can check your spelling later.)

Matt: Hello. Matt Thomas speaking.

Ken: Hello Matt, it's Ken Brown here.

Matt: G'day, Ken. How're you going?

Ken: Not bad, thanks. Look I hear you have an investment project _____ **the pipeline**.

Matt: That's right, yes. You're **quick off the** _____. We've only just re-advertised it.

Ken: Well we're always **on the** _____ **for** good investments and your proposal looks promising **on** _____ . We haven't **gone over the fine** _____ yet though. But I have a few questions if you don't mind.

Matt: Sure. Go ahead.

Ken: I heard there was a company interested in the investment but then the deal _____ **through** before it was **wrapped** _____?

Matt: That's right. The company was keen to **get in on the** _____ but there was **a question** _____ **over** their finances.

Ken: I see.

Matt: They seemed _____ **dinkum** at first but then we realised they were **playing for** _____ and so we **pulled the** _____.

Ken: **I get the** _____. So now you **are back to square** _____?

Matt: Unfortunately yes. And we've wasted a bit of time already which has left us _____ **of pocket** so I'll **be** _____ **front** with you; we are keen to get moving on this.

Ken: Well as I said we're **in the** _____ **for** a good investment...So...

Matt: Well, **you've come to the right** _____ then.

Ken: Mm. **Just the** _____, there'd be some risk involved from what I can see. We'd like to negotiate a lower price?

Matt: Not at this stage. Come on Ken; you know risk is always _____ **and parcel** of this kind of investment but believe me, deals like this one are **hard to** _____ **by**.

Ken: Mm.

Matt: And there are several other companies already interested, so if you **want a** _____ **of the action** you'll have to **be first off the** _____.

Ken: OK I'll talk to my partners and get back to you if we want to go any further. But thanks for your time Matt.

Matt: No worries Ken. Give my regards to Emma.

Ken: Will do. Bye Matt.

> Now check your answers by comparing this page with
> CONVERSATION 1.

In order to become more familiar with these new everyday expressions:

◄◄ **Replay Conversation 1**

    1) Listen and tick the boxes ☑ next to the expressions as you hear them.
    2) Write the definitions you can remember. (Some have been done for you as examples.)
    3) Check your answers by turning to page 132.

☐ (project) in the pipeline.............   <u>(project) that is being planned</u>

☐ quick off the mark ....   _____

☐ on the lookout for ....   _____

☐ on paper ....   _____

☐ gone over the fine print ....   _____

☐ fell through ....   _____

☐ wrapped up............................   _____

☐ get in on the act ....   _____

☐ a question mark over..............   _____

☐ *fair dinkum..........................   _____

☐ playing for time......................   _____

☐ pulled the plug ....   _____

☐ I get the picture ....   _____

☐ are back to square one ....   _____

☐ out of pocket ....   _____

☐ be up front..........................   _____

☐ in the market for...................   _____

☐ you've come to the right place   _____

☐ Just the same.......................   _____

☐ part and parcel ....   _____

☐ hard to come by...................   _____

☐ want a piece of the action ......   _____

☐ be first off the mark..............   _____

LANGUAGE NOTES

  * Fair dinkum is an Australian expression that can be used in various contexts.
    For example, it can be used to describe someone as honest, genuine, eg. 'He's fair dinkum. '
    It can mean, 'Really, is that true?' when said as a question with rising intonation, eg. Fair dinkum?

  * When asked, 'How are you?' people sometimes use the expression, 'I'm not bad thanks',
    as a way of saying, 'I'm OK thanks.'

See more about greetings on page 108

CROSSWORD - LANGUAGE REVIEW

Complete the sentences, choosing from the everyday expressions that are listed below. You can use the clues in brackets ( ) at the end of each sentence to help you. Then complete the crossword using the everyday expressions you have written. One has been done as an example.

out of pocket	fall through	in the market
I get the picture	~~a piece of the action~~	on the lookout
		in the pipeline
back to square one	play for time	part and parcel

ACROSS

1) When we saw how successful the deal was, we wanted <u>a piece of the action</u> too. (to get involved)

3) You've explained very clearly so __ _____ _____ _____. (I understand the situation)

5) We have some exciting travel plans ___ _____ _____. (being planned)

7) Our first idea didn't work so we have to go _____ ____ _____ _____. (to start again)

9) I haven't decided what to do yet, so I'm going to _____ _____ _____. (delay doing it)

Note: The expressions for 8) and 10) are interchangeable, so check where the expressions fit the crossword.

DOWN

2) If you don't want the project to _____ _____, make sure you plan carefully. (fail to happen)

4) It was very expensive so now I'm _____ _____ _____. (have less money than expected)

6) Travelling is _____ ____ _____ of a pilot's job. (a expected part)

8) I'm ____ _____ _____ for a house in this area. (searching, looking for)

10) My car was stolen so I'm ____ _____ _____ for a new car. (interested in buying)

You can check your answers on page 123.

FOCUS ON SPOKEN LANGUAGE

Forming Questions - Review of the 'rules'

Questions in written English generally follow grammar 'rules' which state that:

- Auxiliary verbs such as **Is, Can, Are, Has, Have** or **Do** go *before the subject* :

  For example: Is John here yet?

  subject

  Can you help me?

- When using question words such as **When, Where, Who, What, How, Why**, or **Which**, the question word *goes before the auxiliary verb*.

  subject

  For example: Where are you going?

  Why did he go?

A) Questions in spoken English

In spoken English however, the structure of questions can be different to the general grammar rules above.

For example, in conversational English, questions may be asked in the same word order as statements, then followed by 'if you don't mind' or 'if that's OK'.

1) Check Ken's question in Conversation 1, on page 102 and complete the statement.

   Ken:_____, if you don't mind.

Spoken questions can be asked in the same word order as statements, but with a rising intonation. This happens when we want to confirm something that we think we already know to be true.

In Conversation 1 (page 102) there are examples of questions with the same word order as statements. For example:

'I heard there was a company interested in the investment

but then the deal fell through before it was wrapped up?'

2) Check Conversation 1 for another example of a question with the same word order as a statement.

Answers, page 123

B) Telephone Introductions

When people answer a business telephone call, they generally begin by giving their full name. Notice how the speakers introduced themselves in Conversation 1. Complete the introductions.

Matt: Hello. _____

Ken: Hello _____

Notice Ken said, '...<u>it's</u> Ken Brown here.'
It would also be possible for him to say, 'Hello <u>this is</u> Ken Brown.'
However, when beginning a telephone call, he would <u>not</u> say, 'Hello, <u>I am</u> Ken Brown.'

Note that after the introductions, the speakers in Conversation 1 used less formal language and greetings because they already knew each other as business acquaintances.

FOCUS ON SPOKEN LANGUAGE

C) Incomplete sentences in spoken language

In spoken English, speakers do not always use complete sentences. Words are often left out, if the meaning is clear without using a complete sentence. This aspect of language is referred to in grammar books as '*ellipsis*'.

For example:	**Informal spoken language**	**Complete sentence**
	Leaving already?	***Are you*** leaving already?
	See you soon.	***I will*** see you soon.

Practice

The following incomplete sentences have been taken from Conversation 1 (page 102).
Words have been left out from the beginning of each utterance.
Write the complete sentence on the lines provided below, then check your answers on page 123.

	Informal spoken language	**Complete sentence**
Matt:	Matt Thomas speaking.	_____ Matt Thomas speaking.
Ken:	Not bad thanks.	_____ not bad thanks.
Ken:	Will do.	_____ will do (that).

D) Greetings and replies

* The usual greeting to use on the telephone is 'Hello,...'

In face to face situations, formal greetings are: 'Good morning', 'Good afternoon', 'Good evening', 'Good night' is only used when leaving people.

In face to face situations, less formal greetings are: 'Hello' or 'Hi'.
In Australia, '**G'day**' is an informal way of greeting friends and strangers.

After the greeting, the usual enquiry is:' How are you?'
Less formal enquiries are: 'How're you going?', 'How're things?', 'How's everything?'

* Common replies are: Very well, thank you. ⎤
  Fine, thank you.   ⎬ Formal
  Fine, thanks.   ⎦
  OK, thanks.   ⎤
  Not bad, thanks.   ⎬ Less formal
  Not too bad, thanks. ⎦

E) The Negotiating Process

Negotiating involves a series of actions and strategies taken by the participants in order to achieve a result. A successful negotiating process generally includes the following stages and strategies:

Preparation - Decide your objectives: What do you want to get out of the negotiation?
  Research: What do I need to know about the subject?

Discussion - Begin with a friendly opening.
  Say what you would like to achieve.
  Ask questions to find out more about the situation.
  Listen carefully; if possible take notes.

The Negotiating Process (continued)

Proposing - Make an offer or suggestion. Give an alternative offer or suggestion if you are not satisfied with what is offered to you.
Give reasons for your offer, eg. 'I'm buying a large amount so I'd like a discount.'
Be prepared to trade something. For example say: 'If you..., then we'll ...'
Generally you will receive more if you begin by asking for more.

Closing   - If an agreement is reached, summarise what has been discussed.
For example, say: 'So it's agreed that we'll ... and you'll ...'
In a business situation, confirm in writing as soon as possible.

If an agreement is not reached, leave the way open for future discussions.
eg. 'I'll discuss this with my colleagues and get back to you.'

Always aim to finish in a friendly way.

Of course, not all negotiations are exactly the same but will generally contain some of these strategies.

Matt's and Ken's Negotiation Process

Work with a partner to complete the information about Ken's and Matt's conversation on page 102. Write what each participant did during the negotiations. Use the suggestions in the box to complete the table below. One answer has been completed as an example.

~~wants to buy a good investment~~	wants to sell an investment project
wants to negotiate a lower price	wants a quick sale (he is out of pocket)
says, 'Not at this stage'.	says, 'I'll talk to my partners and get back to you...
says other companies are interested	says there would be some risks involved
says, 'Thanks for your time.'	says, 'No worries,... give my regards to Emma.'

	Matt	Ken
Objectives: What does each participant want?		wants to buy a good investment
Discussion: What does each participant say about the investment project in the discussion stage?		
Closing: As an agreement was not reached, what was said to leave the way open for future negotiations? How did each participant end in a friendly way?		

You can check your answers on page 123.

(Units 7 - 9)

This section reviews some of the expressions that were introduced in Units 7, 8, and 9 and gives you a chance to see what you have remembered.

Look at the pictures on the opposite page and decide what the people are saying by choosing from the expressions below.

Match each picture with an appropriate expression by writing the correct letter in the box next to each expression.

For extra practice, you could write the appropriate expression in the space provided in the picture.

1) I'm sorry. They've pulled the plug on the sale so it's back to square one. ☐

2) Reading between the lines, I think this holiday is better value. ☐

3) There's no point having a chip on your shoulder. You brought this result on yourself. ☐

4) Repairs are part and parcel of owning an old car. You'll always be out of pocket! ☐

5) This pollution is terrible. The government can't keep turning a blind eye to it! ☐

6) It looks OK on paper but I'll go over the fine print just the same. ☐

7) I know you've had a raw deal but you'll get back on your feet soon. ☐

8) The nurse pulled strings to get these crutches for me. ☐

9) I've been on the look out for this type of painting! ☐

Answers: page 123

(Units 7 - 9)

Part 1 - Pre Listening

1. not OK, not acceptable	unacceptable	2. private	personal
3. in a rude way, speaking too directly	abrupt	4. not understand	misunderstand

5. feel worried or ashamed because of something that happened embarrassed

Listening for General Understanding

1) b) they were abrupt and unfriendly

2) a) They offered help.

3) a) why he didn't have children

4) b)) It's considered to be personal and we don't ask those questions.

Part 5 – Crossword

Across:
1. easier said than done
3. jump to conclusions
5. put my foot in it
7. benefit of the doubt
9. have a chat

Down:
2. get the wrong idea
4. in a flash
6. house of fire (housefire)
8. break the ice
10. eyeopen

Part 6 - Focus on Spoken Language

A) Noticing 'weak forms' in spoken English

1) Kara: So how **are** things with **your** neighbours these days Don?

2) Don: **We're** getting on like a house on fire now. It took a while to break the ice but **we're** getting on well now.

3) There are 20 contractions (Note: person's is not a contraction but shows possession.)

B) Pronunciation of *we're, were and where*

Don: **We're** getting on like a house on fire now. It took a while to break the ice but **we're** really getting on well now.

Well they **were** very embarrassed, of course, but they **were** really pleased that we'd explained the situation to them.

Part 6   B) Further Practice – were, where or we're?

1. We're very happy with our English lessons.

2. We visited over ten countries while we <u>were</u> overseas last year.

3. When we <u>were</u> young, we <u>were</u> always in trouble.

4. When we have finished this course, <u>we're</u> going to have a final exam.

5. <u>Where</u> do you come from?

6. Yesterday we <u>were</u> all studying hard for the language tests.

Spelling Practice

1) <u>Their</u> car was stolen while <u>they</u> were away last week, and <u>they're</u> still upset about it.

2) Yesterday we <u>were</u> worried about the exam but now <u>we're</u> happy with our results.

3) <u>Your</u> brother is taller than you, even though <u>you're</u> older than him.

ANSWERS TO UNIT TWO – HOBBIES AND SPORT

Title Page

1	fishing	2	cycling	3	soccer	4	volleyball
5	cards	6	baseball	7	jogging, running	8	horse riding (horse back riding)
9	golf	10	chess	11	cricket	12	tennis

Part 1 - Pre Listening

1) have a strong desire to win <u>be competitive</u>   2) a group of players   <u>a team</u>

3) share in an activity   <u>participate</u>   4) unreasonable, too much <u>extreme</u>

5) having a healthy body   <u>physically fit</u>

Listening for general understanding

A) fishing, jogging, cycling, soccer, cards, chess, cricket, baseball

B) 1) fishing   2) play in a team sport   3) people can be too competitive

Part 5 - Crossword

```
                                                    2
                                                    g
                            4                       e
                        1 t r y * m y * h a n d * a t
              6             i                       *
            3 d o * m y * o w n * t h i n g         i
              r             e                       n
              o             *                       t
              p  5 c o u c h * p o t a t o          o
              *             n                       *
              o             *              8        s
              f             m          7 g i v e * u p      10
              *             y                   n   h        t
              a             *                   w   a        a
              *             h          9 a * r a i n * c h e c k
              h             a                   n   p        e
              a             n                   d            *
              t             d                                u
                            s                                p
```

Part - 6 Focus on Spoken Language

A) Using the correct verb when talking about sport and hobbies

Exercise 1)

play/plays/playing/played		go/goes/going/went/have been		do/does/doing/did/have done	
chess	tennis	jogging	bowling	housework	yoga
cards	soccer	shopping	cycling	pottery	
golf	snooker	bushwalking	skiing	gymnastics	
cricket		fishing	surfing	origami	
		sight seeing	scuba diving	archery	

Exercise 2).

1) I _**play**_ soccer every weekend.

2) We _**went**_ fishing again last weekend.

3) I'd like to _**go**_ bushwalking in the mountains during the holidays.

4) We _**play**_ golf every Saturday afternoon.

5) She _**does**_ yoga every afternoon after work.

6) I think we'll _**go**_ cycling when we go to Amsterdam. It's very flat there.

7) My brother _**does**_ archery as a hobby.

8) Do you know how to _**do**_ origami?

9) We plan to _**go**_ scuba diving when we are on holidays in Queensland.

10) We _**went**_ skiing in the Snowy Mountains last winter.

B) Describing feelings and situations – adjectives ending in 'ed' and 'ing'

1) Look at the pattern, then complete the sentences:

1a) She was amaz*ed* by the story	1b) The story was amaz*ing*
2a) I feel relax*ed* at the beach.	2b) The beach is relax*ing*.
3a) I get bor*ed* at school.	3b) I think school is **boring**.
4a) I get tir*ed* when I study for too long.	4b) It's tir*ing* to study for too long.
5a) I was frighten*ed* by the movie.	5b) The movie was frighten*ing*.
6a) I get excit*ed* when I watch soccer.	6b) I think soccer is exci*ting*.

2) Complete the story below using the correct words from the box.

The sports competition was very _**exciting**_. Everyone in the audience was cheering and clapping. We were all very _**excited**_ when the winner was announced. I was _**amazed**_ to see how fast the competitors could run. Their speeds were _**amazing**_!

The long speeches that followed the competition were a bit _**boring**_. I often get _**bored**_ when people keep talking for a long time. In fact I started to feel so, _**tired**_ I had trouble keeping my eyes open. It was a long and _**tiring**_ day but it was a lot of fun.

Part 1 - Pre Listening

1. a small amount of food that you can eat between main meals	*snack*
2. activities and actions that you do often and regularly	*habits*
3. food that is unhealthy but quick and easy to eat	*junk food*
4. to make someone feel they want to do something	*to inspire*
5 strong control of your thoughts and decisions to do something	*willpower*
6. things that are made to be sold	*products*
7. information put on a product to tell you about the product	*label*
8. people who have a lot of knowledge about something	*experts*

Listening for general understanding

1) b) great (very good)

2) b) goes for a walk

3) b) read the labels on food

Part 5 - Crossword

Across:
- 1. the * works
- 3. so * called
- 5. go * out * the * window
- 7. pay * off
- 9. you * name * it

Down:
- 2. frame * of * mind
- 4. in * no * time
- 6. turn * over * a * new * leaf
- 8. on * the * offside
- 10. workout

Part 6 - Focus on Spoken Language

A) Prepositions such 'on' and 'off' can be used in various ways

Practice   Now I'm feeling <u>on</u> top of the world.   Well the effort has paid <u>off</u>.

…you'll be <u>on</u> the right track   It got me <u>off</u> to a good start.

Part 6 B) Sequencing in story telling

Sentences spoken by the speakers in Conversation 1	Past/present/future
1. You look great!	present
2. I've been on a health kick since the last time I saw you.	past to present
3. Before the diet I was feeling really burnt out.	past
4. Now I'm feeling on top of the world	present
5. You look really great.	present
6. I worked out at the gym in the beginning and it got me off to a good start.	past
7. Now I go for a walk every morning before breakfast	present
8. I eat too much junk food and not enough greens	present
9. But I get bamboozled when it comes to knowing what's best.	present
10. I should start checking labels. *	future
11. I'm heading down that way now... I'll show you.	present to future
12. Well, you've inspired me! *	past - present
13. I'm going to turn over a new leaf.	future
14. And if you like, you can come walking in the mornings. *	future

10. 'should' is used here before a 'present tense verb' to express a tentative action in the future. 'should' is used to show intention of a preferred action in the future.

Note: 'should' can be used to refer to the past when it is followed by a past tense verb.
eg. I should have checked the label (but I didn't).

12. The present perfect tense is used to describe a situation that began in the past and extends to the present (time of speaking), eg,... you've inspired me (since we began speaking to now).

14. 'And if you like, you can come walking in the mornings' is an offer or invitation relating to the future.

C) As the saying goes:

Saying	Meaning
1. Make hay while the sun shines.	a) Do something when you have the opportunity.
2. A problem shared is a problem halved.	c) It can help to talk about a problem with another person.
3. Practice makes perfect.	f) Doing an activity many times makes you do it well.
4. Many hands make light work.	d) If many people help with something, the work will be easier.
5. The proof of the pudding is in the eating.	e) Something can only be judged after it has been tried in a practical way.
6. Don't count your chickens before they're hatched.	b) Don't make definite plans until you've seen how a particular situation develops.

D) When it comes to…
1) Pam: Trouble is, I don't have any will power when it comes to food.
2) Pam: I guess so. But I get bamboozled when it comes to knowing what's best.

It's a matter of…

3) Sara: But really it's a matter of changing your mindset about what's yummy.

1) G   4) F   7) E

2) I   5) H   8) A

3) B   6) D   9) C

ANSWERS TO UNIT FOUR – THE ENVIRONMENT

Part 1 - Pre Listening

1. be involved with people in an activity **participate**   2. a difficult job or situation **a challenge**

3. a duty to do something   **responsibility**   4. use something again   **recycle**

5. an organised activity for a special purpose **a campaign**

Listening for general understanding

1) b) the local river   2) a) more than 30 million

3) a) use less electricity and c) use less water

Part 5 - Crossword

		2										4		6	

Across and down answers:

- 1 across: a * d r o p * i n * t h e * o c e a n
- 2 down: c o m e s * t o t e * c r u n c h (c-o-m-e-s-*-t...)
- 3 across: d o * o u r * b i t
- 4 down: h a n d s * a r e * t i e d
- 5 across: l e n d * a * h a n d
- 6 down: p u l l e d * t o g e t h e r
- 7 across: g e t * b e h i n d
- 8 down: f i x * u p
- 9 across: t a k e * t h e * l e a d
- 10 down: t a k e * p a r t

Part 6 - Focus on Spoken Language

A) The definite article

a) 'This year they're cleaning up the local river.'

b) 'But I don't want to get in the river.'

c) 'Oh there are lots of ways to get behind the campaign…'

d) 'But a few people picking up plastic bags out of the river aren't going to save the world.'

e) 'I've made up my mind to join the Clean Up the World campaign this year.'

Omission of the definite article

f) 'One man, an Australian, Ian Kiernan saw the pollution in Sydney Harbour…

B) Uses of the word 'take'

3) Anyway it's up to the politicians to take the lead on these issues.

4) Ian Kiernan saw the pollution in Sydney Harbour and decided to take up the challenge to clean it up.

5) … now over a hundred countries take part.

Part 6 C) Phrasal verbs

1. 'pull together'   co-operate   2. 'join in' participate in/be involved   } 2. & 4. are interchangeable

3. 'get behind' (an activity) support   4. 'take part be involved/participate   }

D) Describing what is happening

Other sentences are possible but here are some suggestions:

In China, the man and woman are lending a hand to collect rubbish.	Picture 7
The boys are pulling together to plant a tree.	Picture 2
The people are taking part in the Clean Up the World campaign.	All pictures
The people are getting behind the campaign to clean up the beach.	Picture 8
The young boys are doing their bit to clean up the rubbish.	Picture 6
The men are pulling together to clear weeds from the river.	Picture 9
The people are pulling together to pull rubbish from the water.	Picture 5
The people are joining in the Clean Up the World campaign.	All pictures

ANSWERS TO UNIT FIVE – FEARS AND PHOBIAS

Part 1 - Pre Listening - Phobia in each illustration

storms _5_   heights _2_   insects _6_   going in a lift _1_   flying _3_   mice _4_

Correct meanings

1. scared   2. a lift   3. thunder   4. high-rise   5. avoid   6. stuck

Listening for general understanding

1) b) going in lifts   2) b) mice   3) a) storms

Part 5 - Crossword

1 across: creepy * crawlies
2 down: scared * stiff
3 across: work * on * it
4 down: freak * out
5 across: jump * out * of * my * skin
6 down: grin * and * bear * it
7 across: come * clean
8 down: lose * face
9 across: have * a * thing * about
10 down: off * hand
11 across: touch * wood

Part 6 - Focus on Spoken Language

A) Practice My brother‿is‿scared <u>stiff</u>‿of storms. He jump<u>s</u>‿out‿of his‿skin.

B) Word combinations – using the correct preposition

I think most people have a phobia <u>about</u> something. Take my boss - she's got a thing <u>about</u> creepy crawlies and I'm scared stiff <u>of</u> mice – even tiny ones! I freaked <u>out</u> last week when I found out there was a mouse <u>in</u> the office. I was standing <u>on</u> my chair! We had a good laugh <u>about</u> it later.

My brother is scared stiff <u>of</u> storms. He jumps <u>out</u> of his skin every time there's loud thunder. He's working <u>on</u> it though because he doesn't want it to get the better <u>of</u> him.

C) Plural Nouns

Kara is scared of mice.
Don has a thing about lifts.
Kara's brother is afraid of storms.

D) Examples of 'only if …'
1. Yes, but <u>only if</u> I'm with someone and don't want to lose face…
2. <u>Only if</u> I can bring my pet mouse with me!

E) Synonyms

unafraid	*brave*	scared	*frightened*
stupid	*foolish*	embarrassed	*ashamed*
worried	*concerned*	terrible	*awful*
pleased	*glad*	funny	*amusing*

ANSWERS TO UNIT SIX - PEOPLE AND RELATIONSHIPS

Part 1- Listening for general understanding

1) a) her boss keep checking on her
2) b) he was friendly and said, 'Oh I wanted to see you'.
3) a) 'OK. That would be nice.'

Part 5 - Crossword

```
          2
          a
          l    1 o f f * m y * c h e s t
          l                    h(4)             6
          *           3 h a v e * i t * o u t
5 a * g o o d * s p o r t      n                t
          m                    g           8    h
          i                    e           s    e
          l    7 s e e * e y e * t o * e y e    *
          s                    *      10   p    p
                               o      a    a    u
9 c u t * a * l o n g * s t o r y * s h o r t    n
                               *      *    *    c
                               t      h    h    h
                               u      o    e    *
                               n      w    *    l
                               e      *    d    i
                                      o    u    n
                                      f    m    e
11 f u l l * o f * h e r s e l f           m
                                           y
```

Across:
1. off my chest
3. have it out
5. a good sport
7. see eye to eye
9. cut a long story short
11. full of herself

Down:
2. all smiles
4. change our tune
6. the punch line
8. spat the dummy
10. a show of
```
```

Part 6 - Focus on Spoken Language

A) Regular and irregular past tense verbs

bend	_bent_	think	_thought_	are	_were_
keep	_kept_	bite	_bit_	is	_was_
spit	_spat_	go	_went_ (past participle = gone)	catch	_caught_

(See page 75)

C) 'So' and 'Such' used to add emphasis

Kim:… It's been <u>so</u> busy.

Kim: But I thought he was <u>such</u> a show off; and always <u>so</u> full of himself!

Kim: He said he was very taken with my work and that I'd been <u>such</u> a good sport through a very busy time.

ANSWERS TO LANGUAGE REVIEW TWO - UNITS 4 - 6

1) B	4) I	7) G
2) F	5) H	8) E
3) C	6) D	9) A

ANSWERS TO UNIT SEVEN - TALKING ABOUT SOCIAL ISSUES

Part 1 - Pre Listening

1. the opinions and feelings that you have about something — <u>attitude</u>
2. decide or give an opinion about whether something is right or wrong — <u>judge</u>
3. making you feel sad — <u>depressing</u>
4. to <u>not</u> give attention to something — <u>ignore</u>
5. something that helps you do things well and be successful — <u>advantage</u>

Listening for general understanding

1) a) because he likes helping people

2) a) everyone should be responsible for themselves

3) b) people who have advantages should help those who don't (have advantages)

4) a) agree that people should be helped to help themselves

Part 5 - Crossword

1. turn * a * blind * eye
2. look out *for
3. black * and * white
4. upstairs and down
5. down * and * out
6. pick * up *
7. sweep * it * under * the * carpet
8. turn * o * back
9. pull * strings
10. low * bb
11. chip * on * his * shoulder

Part 6 - Focus on Spoken Language

A) Disagreeing Politely (Any of the following are correct answers.)

Yes but don't you think people with problems bring it on themselves...

Yes but that's different, you were sick.

Yes but it's not that simple.

Yes but everyone has ups and downs.

Yes but how did you get another job?

B) As the saying goes:

Saying	Meaning
1) There's no such thing as a free lunch.	c) You can not expect to be given things for nothing as things need to be paid for or worked for.
2) You can't judge a book by its cover.	b) Don't judge someone or something by appearance only because you may be wrong.
3) Every cloud has a silver lining.	a) Every bad situation has a benefit or good side- effect.

C) Reflexive pronouns

1) a) The little boy is too small to feed <u>himself</u>. His mother has to feed him.

b) You'll have to cook dinner for <u>yourself</u> tonight. I'm not going to be here.

2) a) I think everyone should be responsible for <u>themselves</u>.

b) We have to help <u>ourselves</u>.

c) But my point is, wouldn't it be better to help people to help <u>themselves</u>?

D) Asking an opinion with a negative question

1) Well, isn't it depressing spending all day with people who are down and out?

2) Yes but don't you think people with problems bring it on themselves?

3) But my point is, wouldn't it be better to help people to help themselves?

E) Incomplete sentences in spoken language

Karen: Dan I think it's great that you're doing social work <u>but</u>...

Karen is hesitant because she doesn't want to offend Dan but also wants to ask his opinion. She hesitates, hoping Dan won't think she is being impolite.

ANSWERS TO UNIT EIGHT - THE MEDIA

Part 1 - Pre Listening

1. someone who writes information or stories for newspapers or TV   <u>a journalist</u>

2. information that is true   <u>fact</u>   3. not a true story   <u>fiction</u>

4. having power over people <u>powerful</u>   5. showing or uncovering   <u>exposing</u>

6. think/act only on fact, not feelings <u>be objective</u>   7. famous people   <u>celebrities</u>

8. wise, careful and correct <u>responsible</u>   9. less than anything else   <u>least</u>

10. negative points   <u>disadvantages</u>

Listening for general understanding

1) b) exciting stories, getting the answer to problems and exposing a cover-up

2) a) getting information about celebrities just to sell a story.

b) when a situation is difficult to report objectively.

3) a) we shouldn't believe everything we read or see on TV.

Part 5 Crossword

Across:

1 `g e t * t o * t h e * b o t t o m`

3 `a * f i n e * l i n e`

5 `b e n d * t h e * t r u t h`

7 `g e t * a w a y * w i t h * m u r d e r`

9 `r e a d * b e t w e e n * t h e * l i n e s`

Down:

2 `i n * a * b a d * l i g h t`

4 `a * h d d e n * a g e n d a`

6 `s t o p * a t * n o t h i n g`

8 `m n * t h e * w h o l e`

10 `t o e * t h e * l i n e`

Part 6 - Focus on Spoken Language

A) The definite article 'the' - Review

> 1) I like being in <u>the thick</u> of an exciting story; getting to <u>the bottom</u> of a problem.
>
> 2) On <u>the other hand</u>, the media can act as a watchdog, making sure politicians and big business toe <u>the line.</u>
>
> 3) …people have to read between <u>the lines</u> and try to get more than one side to a story.
>
> 4) …some journalists will stop at nothing to make a story interesting even if it means bending <u>the truth</u>.

B) That

Examples

1. 'I hear you're a journalist now Paul. <u>That</u> must be exciting.'
That refers to <u>Paul's job as a journalist.</u>

2. Paul: And <u>that</u>'s why people have to read between the lines.
That refers <u>to the fact that reporters can put a story in a good light or in a bad light.</u> ***and*** <u>The media has a lot of power.</u>

C) Open-ended questions

1. What do you like best about your job?

2. And what do you like least?

D) You get used to it.

Paul: Well yes, <u>you get used to it</u>, but if you feel really strongly about something it's difficult to be objective about it.

E) 'get'

1. Paul: Oh, I like being in the thick of an exciting story; **getting to the bottom of** a problem;

2. Paul: Some organisations or governments would **get away with murder** if the media wasn't keeping an eye on them.

Part 1 - Pre Listening

1. buying something to make a profit later *investment*
2. management of money *finances*
3. the possibility of a bad result *risk*
4. relating to the law *legal*
5. work or activity done over a period of time *project*
6. a business agreement *a deal*
7. suggestion or offer *proposal*
8. honest or real, not false *genuine*

Listening for general understanding

1) b) an investment project 2) a) there are some risks involved with the deal
3) a) There are several companies already interested.

Part 5 - Crossword

	2																		
	f					**4**													
1	a	*	p	i	e	c	e	*	o	f	*	t	h	e	*	a	c	t	i	o	n
	l						u						**6**						
	l		**3**	I	*	g	e	t	*	t	h	e	*	p	i	c	t	u	r	e
	*						*					a				**8**			**10**
	t						o					r				o			i
	h						f					t				n			n
	r						*					a				*			*
	o						p					*				t			t
	u						o		**5**	i	n	*	t	h	e	*	p	i	p	e	l	i	n	e
	g						c					d				*			*
	h						k					*				l			m
							e					p				o			a
			7	b	a	c	k	*	t	o	*	s	q	u	a	r	e	*	o	n	e		o			r
												r				k			k
												c				o			e
			9	p	l	a	y	*	f	o	r	*	t	i	m	e		u			t
												l				t			

Part 6 - Focus on Spoken Language

A) Questions in spoken English

1) ...but I have a few questions , if you don't mind.
2) So now you are back to square one? or
    Actually we'd like to negotiate a lower price?

C) Incomplete sentences in spoken language

Matt: <u>This is</u> Matt Thomas speaking.
Ken: <u>I am</u> not bad thanks.
Ken: <u>I</u> will do (that).

E) The Negotiating Process

Objectives What does each participant want?	wants to sell an investment project wants a quick sale (he's out of pocket)	wants to buy a good investment wants to negotiate a lower price
Discussion: What does each participant say about the investment project in the discussion ?	says other companies are interested	says there would be some risks involved
Closing: What was said to leave the way open for future negotiations? How did each participant end in a friendly way?	says, 'Not at <u>this</u> stage'. says, 'No worries. Give my regards to Emma.'	says, 'I'll talk to my partners and get back to you... says, 'Thanks for your time.'

ANSWERS TO LANGUAGE REVIEW THREE - UNITS 7 - 9

1) C
2) A
3) B
4) D
5) H
6) F
7) G
8) I
9) E

EVERYDAY EXPRESSIONS   DEFINITIONS

how are things…………………………	how is your situation
like a house on fire………………………	like very good friends
break the ice……………………....……	be relaxed and friendly
didn't get off to a good start…………	didn't start well
didn't hit it off………………….………	didn't have a good relationship (when first meeting)
came across as…………………..………	seemed to be or appeared to be
in a flash……………………....….……	very quickly
it dawned on me……………..………..	it became clear to me
get the wrong idea about (someone)	misunderstand
having a chat…………………..………	talking informally
taken aback…....…………………….…	surprised and shocked
overstepped the mark………...……….	behaved in an unacceptable way
the dos and don'ts…………...…………	things you should do and the things you shouldn't do
put our foot in it………………..………	said or done something embarrassing
an eye opener………………..………..	a situation to learn from
jump to conclusions…………..….……	form an opinion before having enough information
easier said than done……………...……	It sounds easy to do but is difficult to do
give (people) the benefit of the doubt	believe people are acting honestly, even if I'm not sure
when all is said and done……………..	when everything is considered

EVERYDAY EXPRESSIONS

DEFINITIONS

EVERYDAY EXPRESSIONS	DEFINITIONS
into (something)	very involved in
take a raincheck	say no to this invitation (but may accept at another time)
(go) at the drop of a hat	(go) willingly and immediately, without hesitation
keep it in mind	I'll remember that
unwind	relax
doesn't do much for me	doesn't interest or excite me
take up (a sport)	start participating in (a sport)
I wouldn't mind	I would like to (try)
to tell you the truth	really, actually, in fact
up to it *	capable or fit enough to do it
give (it) up	quit, stop doing (it)
time on my hands	have some free time available
a couch potato	an inactive, lazy person
get into shape	to become physically fit
try my hand at	try, test my skill at
play by the book	follow the rules
do my own thing	do things the way I want to and be independent
go overboard	become too extreme
full on	too intense, extreme

Note:

* The expression 'take up' (a sport) can be used to talk about other activities, interests or habits that someone starts doing. For example: 'I've taken up cooking', 'He's taken up smoking again.'

* **not** up to (something) means **not** capable or fit enough to do (something)
   For example: 'I'm not up to going to work today. I feel sick.'

EVERYDAY EXPRESSIONS

DEFINITIONS

EVERYDAY EXPRESSIONS	DEFINITIONS
Long time no see!.....................	I haven't seen you for a long time!
health kick.................................	special health program
the works	all things relating to this (topic)
burnt out	very tired
oomph.	energy or excitement
get up and go	energy to do things
on top of the world......................	very well and happy
paid off	has been successful
worked out (at the gym)	exercised your body (at the gym)
got me off to a good start	helped me begin well
good frame of mind	good way of thinking
when it comes to (something).......	with regard to (something)
yummy..	very good to eat
(plans) go out the window	(plans) are forgotten, don't happen
'Old habits die hard'	It's difficult to change habits you've had a long time
mindset	way of thinking, opinions
greens...................................	green vegetables
bamboozled.............................	confused
so called (something).................	incorrectly called (something)
on the right track......................	doing the right thing for success
in no time.................................	very soon, quickly
veggies...................................	vegetables
you name it.............................	and many more things (that I could mention)
turn over a new leaf...................	start doing things in a better way

EVERYDAY EXPRESSIONS	DEFINITIONS
made up my mind	decided
getting together............................	meeting
There's no point............................	There's no good reason or purpose
fix up	repair or improve
a drop in the ocean	a very small amount; not enough for what is needed
it's up to....................................	it's the decision and responsibility of (someone)
take the lead	be an example to other people
Our hands are tied........................	We don't have the power to do anything
when it comes to the crunch	when the situation has become serious
everyone's business	something everyone should know about
pull together	co-operate
get behind (the campaign)..............	support (the campaign)
do our bit....................................	help to do some of the work
It'll take more than that	That will not be enough, it will require more.
lending a hand	helping
joined in	participated, became involved in
take up	begin (doing an activity)
setting up	beginning and preparing (for something)
take part	be involved, participate
point taken	I understand your idea, opinion.
Such as?	What is an example (of that)?

EVERYDAY EXPRESSIONS

DEFINITIONS

EVERYDAY EXPRESSIONS	DEFINITIONS
(a) get-together............................	(an) informal meeting with friends
count you in...............................	include you
I'll pass	I'll say 'no', not accept (the invitation)
come clean (about something)	be honest (about something)
have a thing about (something)*	have a <u>dislike</u> of (something)
lose face	look foolish
get out of doing (something)......	avoid doing (something)
grin and bear it	do something even if I don't want to
hold my breath	wait nervously (for something to happen)
Touch wood	I hope the good situation continues.
take (something or someone)	Take as an example of this (something or someone)
creepy crawlies..........................	insects
scared stiff	very afraid
freaked out	acted strangely because I was afraid
found out...................................	learnt
wasn't fazed	wasn't worried
have a sense of humour	be able to see funny situations in everyday life
jumps out of his skin...............	gets a sudden, bad shock
working on it..............................	trying to improve the situation
(not) let it get the better of you)	(not) let a problem control (you)
mind over matter.....................	the power of your thoughts affecting how you feel
don't let it get out of hand.........	don't let the situation get out of control

* To 'have a thing about' (something) can mean you really <u>don't</u> like something, **or** <u>do</u> like something; depending on the context.

e.g. *She has a thing about spiders. She's scared of them.* = She <u>hates</u> spiders. She's scared of them.
e.g. *He has a thing about motorbikes; he has several of his own.* = He really <u>likes</u> motorbikes.

EVERYDAY EXPRESSIONS

DEFINITIONS

EVERYDAY EXPRESSIONS	DEFINITIONS
had a lot on my plate ………………	had a lot of work to do
on edge………………………………	nervous, not relaxed
(not) get on with……………………	(not) have a good relationship with
from the word go ……………………	from the beginning
*bent over backwards ……………	tried very hard to please (someone)
keeping tabs on (me) ……………..	watching (me and what I was doing)
don't see eye to eye………………	don't agree
spat the dummy ……………………	spoke angrily
bit my tongue………………………	didn't say anything although I wanted to
a show-off …………….… ………..…	a person who tells others he is very good
full of himself ………………..……	pleased with himself & thinks he is so important
Come on, get on with (something)	Hurry, continue with (something; an activity)
That's it! ……………………………	I'm going to deal with this situation!
get this off my chest…………. ….	talk (to someone) about this problem
have it out…………..………………	to talk openly about (a problem) with someone
to cut a long story short …………	I'll tell you only the main part of the story
all smiles…………………………..	look very friendly, happy
caught me off guard ……………..	surprised me (I was not expecting it)
taken with (someone or something)	pleased and impressed with (someone or something)
a good sport………………………..	a pleasant person who doesn't complain
the punch line………………………	the last part of the story that makes it interesting
asked me out………………………	invited me to go out somewhere
you're pulling my leg……………..	you're telling me something that is not true
lost for words………………………	unsure what to say
changed your tune………………..	changed your opinion

* 'bent over backwards' or bent over backward'

EVERYDAY EXPRESSIONS   DEFINITIONS

EVERYDAY EXPRESSIONS	DEFINITIONS
down and out	very poor, with no job
sweep it under the carpet	try to hide or forget about (it)
bring it on themselves	cause the problem for themselves
pick up the pieces	fix the problem after a difficult situation
at a low ebb	feeling depressed, unhappy
get back on my feet	become independent again
'The buck stops here'	'I'm responsible for the result of my decision'
black and white	simple issues of being completely right or completely wrong
ins and outs	all the details
get a raw deal	be treated unfairly
one thing leads to another	one situation causes another situation
can't get out of the rut	can't change the bad situation
a vicious circle	a situation in which one problem creates more problems
ups and downs	good and bad experiences
That's life!	We must accept the things that happen (in our life).
a chip on my shoulder	an angry, resentful attitude
get on with it	continue my usual activities
pulled strings	used influence with important people to get something
looked out for (someone)	helped and cared for (someone)
turn our back on	ignore
a chain reaction	one situation causes another situation
I see what you're getting at	I understand what you're explaining
turning a blind eye	ignoring something because you don't want to do anything about it

EVERYDAY EXPRESSIONS	DEFINITIONS
a buzz ………………………..…	an exciting feeling
drawbacks ………………..……	disadvantages
in the thick of.............................	very involved in
getting to the bottom of.................	finding the answer to
a cover-up. ……………………...	something that has been kept as a secret from people
digging up dirt ………...................	finding bad information (about someone)
(a topic is) close to home…….....	makes me uncomfortable because it affects me personally
touches a nerve............................	is upsetting (for someone)
a fine line between........................	only a very small difference between
a hidden agenda ……………… .	a different meaning to the one openly spoken about
to do with …………….………….	relating to (something)
big business ……………………...	large, powerful companies
a watchdog................................……	a group that makes sure companies act legally
toe the line …………..…..…………	behave in the correct way
get away with murder …….....……	do whatever they want to without control or punishment
keeping an eye on ………………	carefully watching
put it in a good light ……………..	present (the situation) as a good thing
put it in a bad light………………..…	present it as a bad thing
read between the lines..................	understand the *real* meaning, not just what is written or spoken
stop at nothing.........……..……	do anything
bending the truth …………………	saying something that is not completely true
Having said all that ………………	However, in summary
on the whole ………………………	generally
I couldn't have put it better myself.	I agree completely.

EVERYDAY EXPRESSIONS

DEFINITIONS

in the pipeline............................	(something) that is being planned
quick off the mark	quick to act on an opportunity
on the lookout for........................	searching for
on paper	as a plan (but may not show the complete situation)
gone over the fine print	checked the important legal information
fell through	failed to happen
wrapped up	completed, finalised
get in on the act	get involved in the activity
a question mark over (something)	doubt about (something)
fair dinkum	genuine, honest, truthful
playing for time.........................	delay doing anything while deciding what to do
pulled the plug	stopped the deal from continuing
I get the picture	I understand the situation
back to square one	have to start again
out of pocket	with less money than we should have
be up front................................	clear and honest
in the market for (something).......	interested in buying (something)
You've come to the right place.....	We have what you are looking for.
Just the same............................	however
part and parcel	an expected part of (something)
hard to come by........................	difficult to find
want a piece of the action	want to get involved in this activity
be first off the mark....................	act more quickly than anyone else

Phonemic Chart of English Sounds

Below each sound symbol are examples of words containing the sound.

Vowel sounds

æ (short sound)	e (short sound)	ɒ (short sound)	ə (unstressed sound)
bl**a**ck	r**e**d	…. d**o**ts ….	oth**e**r broth**e**r
ɑː (long sound)	ʊ (short sound)	ʌ (short sound)	I (short sound)
c**ar**	g**oo**d	f**u**n	p**i**nk
3ː (long sound)	uː (long sound)	ɔː (long sound)	iː (long sound)
p**ur**ple	bl**ue**	f**our** m**ore**	gr**ee**n

Diphthong (two vowel) sounds

eI	ɔI	əʊ (also oʊ)	Iə
gr**ey**	b**oy**	yell**ow** g**o**ld	cl**ear** b**eer**
eə (also ɛə)	aI	ʊə	aʊ
h**air**	br**i**ght l**i**me	t**ou**r	br**ow**n m**ou**se

Consonant sounds

p	b	t	d
pet **p**ig	**b**ig **b**ag	**t**ell **t**wo	**d**irty **d**og
tʃ	dʒ	k	g
Chinese **ch**ild	**j**ust **j**oking	**k**eep **c**ool	**g**ood **g**irl
f	v	θ	ð
fill **f**our	**v**ery **v**ivid	**th**ink **th**in	o**th**er bro**th**er
s	z	ʃ	ʒ
sad **s**ong	**z**ig-**z**ag	**sh**ort **sh**eep	mea**s**ure A**s**ia
m	n	ŋ	h
milk **m**an	**n**o **n**ever	lo**ng** so**ng**	**h**ot **h**ill
l	r	w	j
little **l**ine	**r**ice	**w**et **w**inter	**y**es **y**ou

As the pronunciation of some English vowel sounds varies across and within countries, the examples given on this chart are intended as a general guide

Boyer Educational Resources books and audio CDs

'Understanding Everyday Australian' – series (books with audio CD)

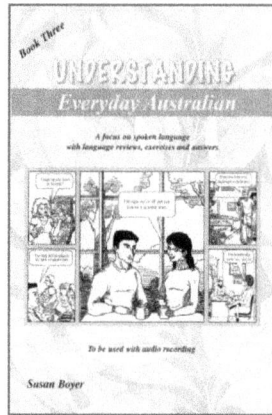

Readers (A5), Audio CDs, Language workbooks

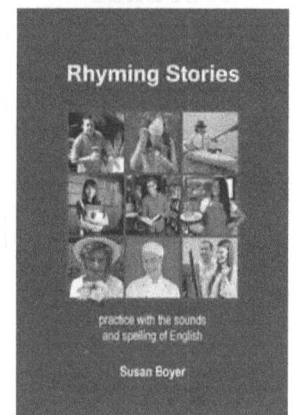

Rhyming Stories — practice with the sounds and spelling of English — Susan Boyer

'Understanding Spoken English' – (books with audio CD) international editions

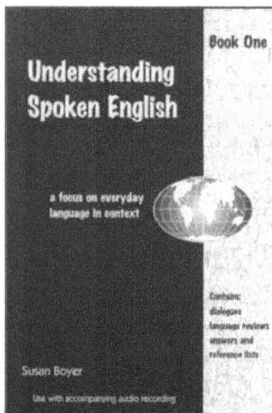

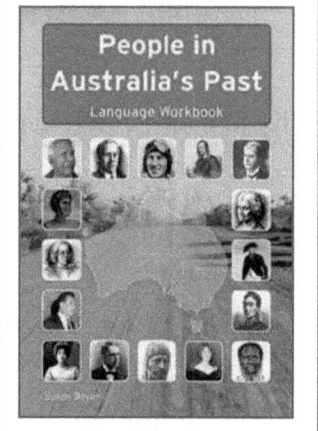

People in Australia's Past — Language Workbook — Susan Boyer

Spelling and Pronunciation for English Language Learners	Understanding English Pronunciation	Word Building Activities for beginners of English	English Language Skills Level One

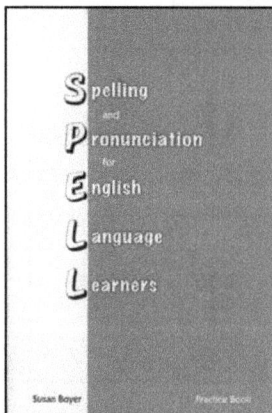

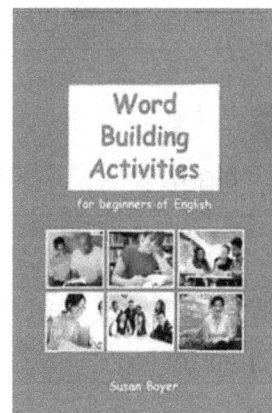

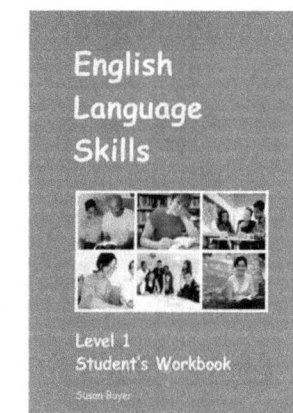

Spiral bound Teacher's Books with photocopiable activities such as surveys, role-cards & matching activities:

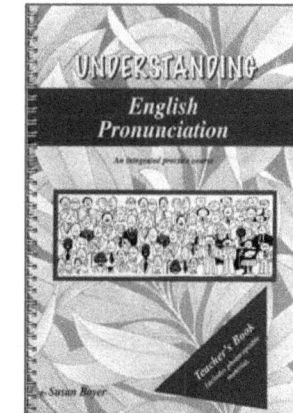

All our teacher's books are A4 size. Student's books contain language exercises and answers.

Boyer Educational Resources

Office phone/fax: +61 (0)2 4739 1538
websites: www.boyereducation.com.au

e-mail: boyer@eftel.net.au
www.englishebooks.com

Title	ISBN	RRP
People in Australia's past - their stories, their achievements - A5 Reader	978 1 877074 34 9	$12.95
People in Australia's past - audio CD	978 1 877074 35 6	$19.95
People in Australia's past - language workbook A4 (156 pages)	978 1 877074 36 3	$44.95
Understanding Everyday Australian - Book One	978 0 958539 50 0	$29.95
Understanding Everyday Australian - Audio CD One (1)	978 1 877074 01 1	$19.95
Understanding Everyday Australian - Teacher's Book One	978 0 958539 52 4	$44.95
Understanding Everyday Australian - Book One & Audio CD	**978 1 877074 16 5**	**$39.95**
Understanding Everyday Australian - Book Two	978 0 958539 53 1	$29.95
Understanding Everyday Australian - Audio CD Two (1)	978 1 877074 02 8	$19.95
Understanding Everyday Australian - Teacher's Book Two	978 0 958539 55 5	$44.95
Understanding Everyday Australian - Book Two & Audio CD Pack	**978 1 877074 17 2**	**$39.95**
Understanding Everyday Australian - Book Three	978 1 877074 20 2	$29.95
Understanding Everyday Australian - Audio CD Three	978 1 877074 21 9	$19.95
Understanding Everyday Australian - Teacher's Book Three	978 1 877074 22 6	$44.95
Understanding Everyday Australian - Book Three & Audio CD	**978 1 877074 23 3**	**$39.95**
Word Building Activities for Beginners of English	978 1 877074 28 8	$29.95
English Language Skills - Level One Student's Workbook	978 1 877074 29 5	$19.95
English Language Skills - Level One Audio CD	978 1 877074 31 8	$19.95
English Language Skills - Level One Teacher's Book	978 1 877074 32 5	$49.95
English Language Skills - Level 1 Teacher's Book & Audio CD	978 1 877074 33 2	$59.95
Rhyming Stories - practice with the sounds and spelling of English (A5)	978 1 877074 06 6	$19.95
Rhyming Stories -audio CD	978 1 877074 37 0	$19.95
Rhyming Stories - language workbook (A4)	978 1 877074 38 7	$29.95
Spelling and Pronunciation for English Language Learners	978 1 877074 04 2	$19.95
Understanding English Pronunciation - Student book only	978 0 958539 57 9	$29.95
Understanding English Pronunciation - Audio CD (Set of 3)	978 1 877074 03 5	$39.95
Understanding English Pronunciation - Teacher's Book	978 0 958539 59 3	$44.95
Understanding Spoken English - Book One	978 1 877074 08 0	$29.95
Understanding Spoken English - Audio CD One (1)	978 1 877074 10 3	$19.95
Understanding Spoken English - Teacher's Book One	978 1 877074 11 0	$44.95
Understanding Spoken English - Book One & Audio CD	**978 1 877074 18 9**	**$39.95**
Understanding Spoken English - Book Two	978 1 877074 12 7	$29.95
Understanding Spoken English - Audio CD Two (1)	978 1 877074 14 1	$19.95
Understanding Spoken English - Teacher's Book Two	978 1 877074 15 8	$44.95
Understanding Spoken English - Book Two & Audio CD	**978 1 877074 19 6**	**$39.95**
Understanding Spoken English - Book Three	978 1 877074 24 0	$29.95
Understanding Spoken English - Audio CD Three	978 1 877074 25 7	$19.95
Understanding Spoken English - Teacher's Book Three	978 1 877074 26 4	$44.95
Understanding Spoken English - Book Three & Audio CD	**978 1 877074 27 1**	**$39.95**

Focus on Australian content · Beginner English · Pronunciation & Spelling · Focus on 'International English'

'Across Great Divides: True stories of life at Sydney Cove'

is a non-fiction narrative which brings to life the experiences of convicts aboard the First Fleet. The stories show varied responses to their unique situation in Australia's first colony.

The stories also give voice to the dilemma of the Aboriginal people challenged by the unexpected arrival of a completely alien race of white people to their land.

Yet meetings between the cultures would be dynamic and varied. The mystery of a new world had begun and the lives of all involved would never be the same again.

***

Susan is available for library and school visits to talk about the stories in her book.

See links to the Australian curriculum at www.birrong books.com

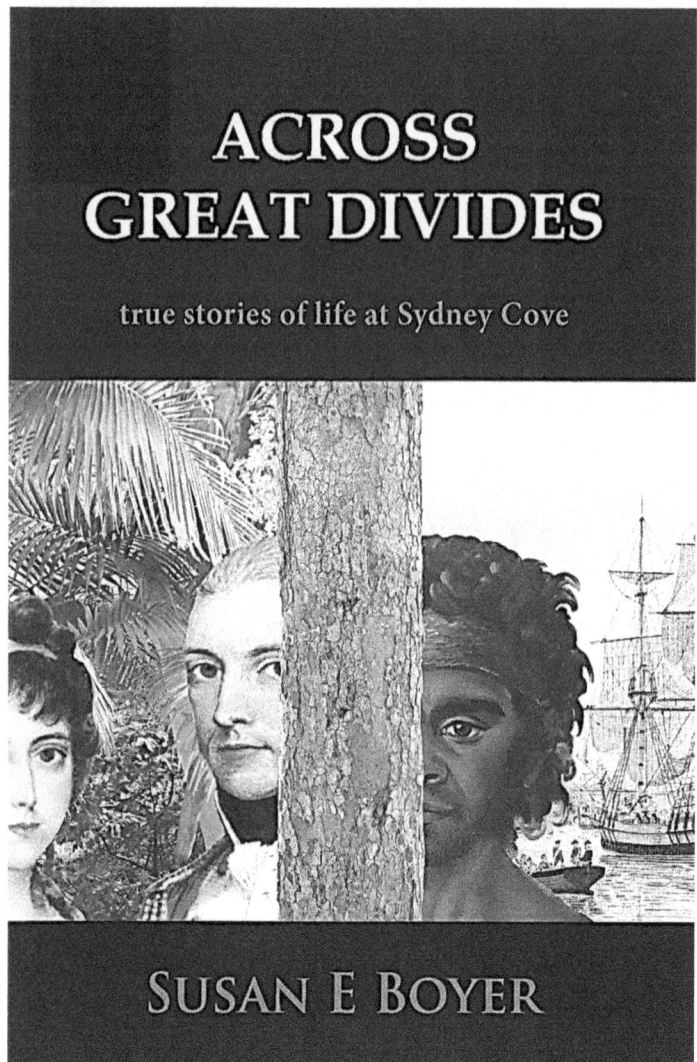

ACROSS GREAT DIVIDES

true stories of life at Sydney Cove

SUSAN E BOYER

A teacher's feedback following Susan's author talk at Windsor Library, NSW (where school students attended)

Hi Susan,
Our kids loved it. They were very engaged and came out saying they wanted more, which was just how my colleague and I felt! Their understanding was clear and I don't think you need to change anything for this level at school. I was very proud of how involved and interested they were. Let us know if you do any more please!
Regards,
Julie Tuck, Year 5/6 teacher, Windsor Public School, NSW, September 2014

***

A reader's feedback following an author talk at Blaxland Library, NSW, May 2014.

Dear Susan,
I thoroughly enjoyed the book, I loved the way it was written and particularly liked that there were enough characters, but it was always easy to keep track of them. Another comment is the easy style of writing you have used. As I said I thoroughly enjoyed the book and I look forward to a future one.
Best regards,
Lachlan

'Across Great Divides: True Stories of Life at Sydney Cove'
Non-fiction Australian history - RRP $26.95
Available at bookstores across Australia or online at
www.birrongbooks.com
Free teaching resources and activities available at the above website

---